The Other Side

What Is the Point of Holding On?

SETH RAMEY

WESTBOW
PRESS®
A DIVISION OF THOMAS NELSON
& ZONDERVAN

WestBow Press books may be ordered through booksellers or by contacting:

WestBow Press
A Division of Thomas Nelson & Zondervan
1663 Liberty Drive
Bloomington, IN 47403
www.westbowpress.com
1 (866) 928-1240

ISBN: 978-1-5127-7973-8 (sc)
ISBN: 978-1-5127-7974-5 (hc)
ISBN: 978-1-5127-7972-1 (e)

Library of Congress Control Number: 2017904253

Print information available on the last page.

WestBow Press rev. date: 03/23/2017

To Tabitha Embrey—sister, fighter, encourager.
You are the epitome of strength. I love you.

Contents

Acknowledgments

Many people helped me write this book, but before I go any further, I would be remiss not to give God all the credit and for drawing me closer to Him through this process. This was as much for me as it was for all of you.

I thank my incredible family for sticking with me through all the hard times. We are a large clan, so I will not name every single one of us, but you all the shoulders on which I lean.

To my adopted brother Brandon and brother-in-law Daniel, thank you for all the encouraging conversations, comedy relief, deep personal friendship, and faith in me.

To my pastor and youth pastor, thank you for all the friendship, biblical knowledge, honest answers, and the time you took from your extensive schedules to listen to me.

To my great friends, Brother Kenny and Sister Courtney, thank you for not only responding to me but being completely real with me whenever I vented to you at 3:00 a.m. Many of those conversations ended up into my book, and I can't thank you enough.

To my beautiful church family, who in the darkest times supported my family and encouraged me to keep going when I wanted to give up on this, thank you.

Thank you to the pillars of my church and our faith for lighting the way.

Thank you to some very dear friends (you know who you are) who went out of their way to become a second family and those very close friends who continue to stand with me.

Last but not least, to my four beautiful nieces, thank you for giving me something to do during my moments of writer's block and for being my favorite girls alive! Without all of you, this book would not exist.

Introduction

My goodness, life sure can throw us headfirst into storms, can't it? When we least expect it. When we are most unprepared. When we are lonely and vulnerable and broken. When we feel that not even God can hear us or help us. It is then, in the midst of the storm, that we are left with these questions: what is the point in holding on? Why don't things add up? What lies on the other side, God? And here we are—taking these questions to a God we assume is nowhere to be found. We've all done it. We deny His ability to stop the storm. We deny His wisdom to answer these questions. But, in our most desperate moments, we still call out to the One that the winds and waves obey, and deep, deep down, we must still trust that He works all things for our good. Even when things are not good to us, they are always good for us.

An introduction is supposed to explain what the book is about, so this is it: we've all faced terrible times in our lives, and perhaps we will face more storms. I have faced questions in my life and taken them to God; no doubt, many of us have done this. We've all asked, in our weariness, what is the point in holding on? All of us have different storms or trials, all of our "other sides" are different, and we've all felt as though there is a gap between God's promises and where we are—as if the distance from shore to shore is too far apart. Now, I don't claim to know the answers to these questions. I can't tell you why you're walking through the storm. I can't tell you how long you have to stay in it, and I can't tell you why your heart is unsettled. I don't have a twelve-step program, and I cannot see your future. I honestly wish I could. It would make everything easier and I would find no greater honor than to be able to help you. But I know someone who's already been there, and I do know what to do in the meantime. The Bible is full of stories that we can use to guide us through these moments.

I wrote this book to encourage you to cling to God, His promises, and His miracles even when those promises and miracles look unlikely. In this book, I will share with you the things that encouraged me during my storm. My desire is to meet you on a personal level and steer you onward. I pray this book blesses you the way it did me when I wrote it.

Section 1

What Is the Point of Holding On?

When thou passeth through the waters, I will be with thee; and through the rivers, they shall not overflow thee ...

—*Isaiah 43:2 (KJV)*

Chapter 1

When God Says "Get In"

"And straightway Jesus constrained his disciples to get into a ship, and to go before him unto the other side, while he sent the multitudes away."

—*Matthew 14:22 (KJV)*

As I studied this scripture, I wondered why Christ told His disciples to get in the boat. No doubt, He knew a storm was coming. He knew they would be in the middle of the water—panic-stricken, probably drenched in water, terrified, broken, confused, and fighting for their lives. Yet there Jesus was, telling them to get in the boat as He went alone to a mountain to pray. Why did He do this? What kind of friend or Messiah would do such a thing? Who would leave His people when things were going so wonderfully and when they were about to get so rough?

We have all been there. We've all asked, "God, why are you thrusting me into this boat that you are not in, and why did you leave?" Or perhaps we asked: "Why are we going to the other side without you?" We've watched God do great things in our lives. We were there when He healed people and provided financial help to our friends at church. We were there when He was feeding the hungry, the church was growing, and His spirit was moving. We were there when the blessings kept coming in our own lives.

Oh, how wonderful it was! Watching God bless us, perform miracles, and plant beautiful things in our lives. Then, seemingly

1

out of the blue, God launched us out into the deep on our own. He told us to get into the boat and to go. How crushed we are to not feel Him like we did before. To no longer see the things we did before. To wonder in our minds why He no longer walks with us. To feel that emptiness and void that He once filled. To feel so unsafe.

In late 2012, my sister was diagnosed with cancer for the first time. She was a wonderful person, one of my best friends. God blessed her and her wonderful husband with four beautiful daughters, my wonderful nieces. Life was perfect. Holidays were exciting. Our family was growing. Every moment together was an incredible memory. Things outside of my family were great as well. Everything was coming together perfectly, it seemed.

But during while she was pregnant with their fourth daughter, doctors found a cancerous tumor on her hand. They assumed, at first, that the tumor was benign. But as time went on, and we uncomfortably waited for test result after test result, and as the birth of my niece drew closer and closer, the good news, comfort, and companionship that we had grown so accustomed to vanished with the news that it was indeed cancerous. Within days of my niece's birth and the addition of a beautiful life, my sister lost her hand. Just like that, my family was thrown into our metaphorical boat.

Mine is not the only family that will be pushed into a boat. We all will be put in one sooner or later. I urge you not to confuse the boats we are often put into with the storms that we go through. Our boats, though scary and dangerous, are often simply the vessels that take us into the storm. But, more important, they take us to the other side.

Why did Jesus tell His disciples to get in the boat? Many have debated about this, and I myself have often wondered. Were the disciples too comfortable where they were and in need of a change of scenery? Did they need a little faith building? Perhaps Jesus had something better prepared for them on the other side. But could it be that His plan was threefold? We will explore that in the following chapters, but rest assured, God knows what He is doing and what we need.

I know in our hearts we know that. I believe the disciples even knew in that moment, but human nature got in the way. They, just like us, were so accustomed to Jesus, their friend, that they lost touch with Jesus, their savior, the sovereign one, the healer, the provider, the deliverer, the restorer. The man who fed multitudes exceedingly and abundantly.

If we are not careful, we may subconsciously humanize God, even after unimaginable miracles. It is in that moment of limiting God that doubt and fear trickle into our lives. It is normal. We are human, and our emotions are often agents of circumstance. Oh, how much would change if we only learned to cling to God—not who He was when He accomplished those things but who He remains. How different things would be if we chose to cling to His promises and His word.

Imagine with me the dialogue the disciples might have had as Jesus abruptly ended the feast with more than five thousand people. I imagine Jesus looked at His disciples and patted them on the back, saying, "All right, boys, get in the boat, and head on over to the other side. I need some time to pray alone, but I'll be there later."

One of the disciples probably would have said, "Wait a minute, Jesus. Do you remember the last time you told us to go to the other side? We got in the boat, and you were there too, and that storm came."

And another disciple stepped in. "Yeah, Jesus, don't you remember? The waves crashed so hard into the boat as it rocked back and forth that it was filled with water, and you were sleeping. That happened with you on the boat, and now you expect us to go without you? No way."

You won't find that dialogue in scripture, but I imagine questions were asked. *Why now?* they probably wondered. They probably feared life without Jesus. Perhaps they feared every moment He wasn't around. Yet there Jesus was, telling them to get in and go to the other side. There were the disciples, hesitantly stepping in, uncomfortable though it might have been. The humor God seems to have is funny to me. We see ourselves in a situation that was similar to a previous experience, one that was far out of our own control. We remember the problems we faced and were grateful that He brought us out. We remembered the doubts and the worry and vowed to never experience that again. Then Jesus comes along and says "Get in. I want you to go through this again."

We often assume that it will be the same old storm and the same old letdown as the last time we stepped in the boat. We always expect the same results. But I believe that God takes us through the storm once to prepare us to go through it again. He has a new experience, a reason, and something of great value for us on the other side. Our doubts and our fears are once again formed by us humanizing God, growing accustomed to Him simply being our friend and neglecting His sovereignty as Savior. It's us being focused solely on the unknown. He truly knows what we need, and He knows how to get us to it.

Again I ask, why did Jesus tell His disciples to get in the boat? Why is He asking you, and how are you responding?

This is a difficult question to answer. But if we listen closely enough, God will give us subtle details that can comfort us along the way. If we can block out the distractions of doubt and worry and focus solely on His whispers, we will see that He is guiding us and speaking to us. Could it be that the same reasons God told the disciples to get in the boat are the ones He has for you? Are you too comfortable where you are and in need of a change of scenery? Are you in need of a little faith building? Perhaps Jesus has something better prepared for you on the other side. If you're wondering why I think those three things could be the reasons they were asked to get in the boat, let me take you back to what happened before they got in the boat.

Chapter 2

More Than the Sum

"And he commanded the multitude to sit down on the grass, and took the five loaves, and the two fishes, and looking up to heaven, he blessed, and brake, and gave the loaves to his disciples, and the disciples to the multitude. And they did all eat, and were filled: and they took up of the fragments that remained twelve baskets full."

—*Matthew 14:19–20 (KJV)*

Before I speak to you about the power of these scriptures and explain the direction I'm going, I must take you farther back to the very beginning of Matthew 14. In the very early verses, we read that Jesus has learned about the death of John the Baptist. His own family member has died. Yet scripture doesn't say Jesus is sorrowful. It doesn't say Jesus dwelled on it, shed a single tear, or even walked with His head hanging down—although I'm sure He felt the pain of loss after His cousin was beheaded. The scripture simply says that when He heard the news, He left by boat and headed to a desert place. I'm sure His intentions were to get away and pray to His Father.

We don't know how much time went by, but eventually Jesus made it to His destination. Along the way, He had accumulated a following of people. Scripture doesn't say why they were there or what they wanted. But clearly they had heard about Him and loved Him. No doubt He loved them too. He cast His own brokenness aside and was moved with compassion for them. He healed them. Loved them. Built relationships with them. Was that not enough? He was heading to a place where He could be alone, a place where He could heal and recover and rest. But He averted His attention to people who needed Him.

They didn't know Him, not in the sense of a relationship. They knew of Him. I'm sure they'd heard His name, but they didn't know Him—not yet anyway. How unselfish the Son of God truly is. Here Jesus was, broken-hearted; weary; mentally, physically, and spiritually exhausted; probably trying to get away and pray. Yet He was healing their sick, talking with them, walking with them, building relationships with them. He delayed all of His plans to meet their needs!

Surely Jesus did His part. Surely He'd done enough. His disciples certainly thought so. He was there all day healing the sick. Touching them. Loving them. He could have left, and I don't think one person there would have been angry with Him. They would have understood. But He was there so long that His own disciples (maybe for their own selfish reasons) made excuses to get the crowds to leave.

"They're hungry, Jesus! Send them away to eat," they said. But Jesus always knows what we need, and He will do what it takes to get us to it. He looked back at His disciples and said, "They don't need to leave. Give them something to eat. Feed them!" Just like man has always done and we always will do, the disciples gave an excuse. We limit God. We compartmentalize Him and throw Him in a box. But Jesus always proves that our assessments of Him are wrong. He does things not only in a greater way, but in a way we never envisioned. And there is never any doubt that He has exceeded all our expectations. The disciples looked at Him and responded, "We have here only five loaves and two fish."

Let me ask you a question. How often do we look at our current circumstance and find excuses for why God can't fix something or why He can't move on our behalf? We think it's too hopeless, too far-fetched. We cannot see it, so we do not believe it. But Jesus was not finished! He had the answers, and He had the way. Jesus looked back at His disciples and said, "Bring them to me," because He had more to do. Every time Jesus tells us to do something, it's because He has something to show us. (Peter would soon learn this, and we will touch on that later.)

I imagine the disciples were perplexed at the situation. "Jesus, I know you and we have walked with you for years, but how on Earth are you going to feed all these people? The food we need makes it impossible. What, are you going to feed them breadcrumbs? You're smart, Jesus. Surely you know that breadcrumbs will not sustain their desires and their needs. Why don't you ask us to go fishing again and cast our nets on the other side?"

But Jesus did, and often does, His best work in the midst of doubts and questions. Knowing this doesn't give us a right to doubt or question God, but He always proves to us that He is always faithful. In this instance, He could see that the food they had didn't look like much, and that to some, things looked hopeless.

Jesus knew better, though. He knew there was more than meets the eye. He looked up to the Creator who had spoken those fish into existence and offered what He did have. As a result, He didn't just feed the crowds of people, he fed them to satisfaction. He healed them, nurtured them, and befriended them. Those two fish and five loaves became twelve baskets full for a lucky child, his family as well as the crowd. Beyond even that, Jesus gave his disciples and the multitudes insight into whom the Son of God is. Jesus truly loves His people, and He would never lead them astray or starving, struggling, or alone—not when they desire Him so much.

Indeed, little is much when God is involved, and those breadcrumbs that we often assume God will give us become an overabundance, more than enough, above and beyond. He provides more than the sum and more than what's necessary, and He will return more than what we offer to Him. God always gives more and blesses more than the sum of what we have or see. He will do more than we ever imagined. And all of those questions and doubts we've had will finally find their answers, through the act of God.

It's a wonderful and beautiful thing to know Jesus loves us enough to deny Himself so he can meet us where we are. But don't let these loaves of bread and fish limit your life like the disciples so quickly and easily did. Even after all of the wonderful things He did, as described in this scripture, they ultimately doubted Jesus that very night.

But the loaves of bread and these fish are simply metaphors for your needs. Do you no longer have hope that you will be healed? Is your marriage crumbling? Does it seem that restoration never will be fulfilled? Is your church dying spiritually? Perhaps your financial state looks an awful lot like the bread and fish, i.e., there is not enough to feed your family and not enough to meet your needs.

If so, could it be that all you need to do is offer up the sum of what you have to God, and then watch as He makes something out of nothing while you seek Him with all your might? This is so often when God moves: when it seems hopeless, when we cannot see or understand how He will do it. We don't know when or how He will move on our behalf. But He always does!

Trust in Him. Run to Him. Cling to Him. Watch as He works on your behalf and always remember it. Soon, He will ask you to get in your boat and head over to the other side. And everything that you thought you knew and all you thought you had will be replaced with confusion, worry, and doubt. All the safety and security you had will seem to leave or cease. Things may look dark, dangerous, and scary as the storm clouds start rolling in.

But thank God, this is not where the story ends. It is merely the beginning. It is the place from where everyone begins the journey into the dangers and terrors of the storm, but it too is the beginning of God's incredible plan for our lives.

Chapter 3

When the Storm Comes

"But the ship was now in the midst of the sea, tossed with waves: for the wind was contrary."

—Matthew 14:24 (KJV)

Often, the storm seems to come out of nowhere. It throws us off guard, totally unprepared. Here we are—obedient to God, adhering to His direction, calm and peaceful, perhaps even comfortable. Yet, just as we begin to obey and move forward in and with Christ, everything is turned upside down. Everything goes completely wrong. This was the case at this point in time. No doubt the disciples were professional fisherman. They'd faced previous storms. Some of them had grown up on the water. But even the strongest in faith and the strongest in Christ will face times that seem far too big and far too overwhelming. Destruction seems to come from every side.

There can be great cause for concern in these moments, even more so when we do not know or cannot find the Maker of the wind, or do not see the end of it or find a way out. We don't always have the answers or the reasons for these storms. Sometimes, we must simply go through them and endure, hold on for dear life as we are rocked back and forth. The disciples were at that point. No doubt they were angry because Jesus was gone, while the winds blew their sails too hard and the waves crashed into the boat, filling it with water. Perhaps they wondered once again about the motives behind Jesus's actions, or whether he had motives at all.

They tried to survive, to cling to hope in the middle of despair, as they bailed buckets of water out of their splintering boat. Meanwhile, the Savior who was supposed to work on their behalf and to save them was off on His own. I am sure we have all been there, when it seems God is absent although we desperately need Him. When my sister was diagnosed with a rare form of cancer, people walked away when we needed them most, and everything else seemed to fall apart around us. It was easy to feel despair. It was easy to be overwhelmed. It was easy to feel rejected and forgotten.

That is precisely what the storms want, though. That is exactly where they want to be, in the forefront of our lives. They always have an agenda. Storms have minds of their own. They want your all, and they want you to be in awe. They want you to give up and give in and to be astonished at their power. Above all, they want to be the ones that sound out the voice of God and for us to be solely focused on them—shaking in our boots, terrified at the thought of what they can do. They want us to neglect His power and sovereignty. The truth is, if we are not careful, it can become easy to do just that and often, that is exactly what happens.

In this particular story, the storm seemed to be victorious. The winds were boisterous. The waters were freezing. The waves were frightening. It was getting late, and it seemed as though God's power and all of His previous works had been nullified. It was as though the disciples had forgotten what Jesus had done and what He had promised—the other side. Based on what we read in Matthew 14, not one time during this storm did they pray or encourage one another. They didn't even yell out to God for help. They were solely and completely focused on the storm.

Now, it is easy for us to look at this story, nitpick at the disciples' actions, and call them out on their doubt, their forgetfulness, their fear. But if we could switch places with them and if we check our own hearts, we will realize that we are not much different. We question God when we should trust in Him. We focus on the storm and forget the other side when that is all we should be

11

looking for. We worry about what might happen and forget His promises. Just like the disciples, when everything is splintering away around us, we simply try to stay afloat. But God wants us to be more than just afloat. He doesn't want us to be comfortable where we are because He has so much more for us. However, sometimes it takes a storm to get us there.

As I was thinking about this chapter, I remembered the lyrics of that song "I Held On":

> You ask me how it is that I'm still standing,
> You ask me how I made it through the storm,
> I can't boast of any special powers,
> I just held on, 'til the storm was over.

And there is no doubt, there are times when all we can do and all we must do is endure and hold on, white-knuckled, until Jesus shows up, in the way this song describes so beautifully. Like the disciples, we may have times of doubt. Like the disciples, we may get scared. Like the disciples, we may feel defeat is knocking on the door. There will be moments when the storm will seem to be victorious as we are swept up in its power.

But it is just like the enemy to come by and say "The darkness is coming. The storm is here. But where is Jesus? Where is your Savior in all of this?" I imagine the disciples asked themselves these questions and, again, we've all been there. But the disciples should have known! Although they couldn't see Him, they should have known that even when He isn't seen or felt, Jesus never changes.

They should have trusted that He would make His presence known. They had walked for years with Him, left all they had behind. They loved Jesus, and they desired to walk the same path that He'd trod. They trusted him enough to follow where He led; yet they did not have the faith in the midst of this storm that He would be faithful to the end, according to His promise. They should have known! Instead, they neglected who He was.

This is the amazing thing. What the enemy plans for evil, God uses for His good, and while the storm wants our all, Jesus will, one way or another, get our full attention. In turn, He will give us, His attention. He will give us Himself and fulfill His Word. While storms are intended to derail us and throw us off course, God uses all kinds of things to fulfill His plans and guide us to the destination He has chosen for us. Let us not fall in to the same trap as the disciples. As the storm raged on and everything grew darker, they were afraid, because they could not see the end. I have been there when I believed God promised me something before the storm came and as it hit, the waves of destruction seemed to have all been crashing in at once. No doubt you either have or will experience this yourself. That is when we must cling to the Rock! Believe on His promises. To believe that He is a God that cannot lie.

In my case, when cancer seemed to take over my life, stress strained relationships, and everything that seemed good fell apart. I began to doubt everything He'd said and promised to me. His promises seemed to be slipping through my fingers like sand. I asked myself why I was holding onto what was already slipping out of my grasp?! What a storm to endure. The wait for help or restoration and standing in the midst of the unknown, wondering if it will ever come true is what most often causes heartache to root up inside of you. That was certainly the case for me, as I am sure it was for the men in the boat. They doubted the words God spoke. Perhaps they considered the fact that they might have misinterpreted God's promise regarding the other side, like we so often do as we try and find any reason to doubt it.

Luckily, the thing that keeps me going—and perhaps what keeps you going—is that God has seen the end from the beginning. He has looked it over, and He will guide you there. Even when we cannot see it, He has already figured a way out of your storm. The call of God involves change. That is why He called the disciples to the other side. And His call leads you on a journey into the unknown and often into the uncomfortable. But do not lose heart when the storm strikes, because even though the enemy intends it for your hurt, God will use it for your benefit.

Perhaps the disciples were in need of a faith building. Even when they could not see and feel Jesus, His power was still prevalent. Perhaps He was preparing them for life on the other side and life after the cross. Maybe He was showing them that, regardless of how hard things get, His promises and divine intervention still remain.

So, when the storm comes, hold on to Jesus's words. Cling to them, and never let the noise and sight of the storm distract you from His promise. Let God use the storm to purge you of all your weaknesses and prepare you for His promises.

The answers to the questions at the end of chapter 1 are these:

1) The disciples seemed comfortable about what Jesus did and where they were. They were content about Jesus feeding the five thousand, as if it were all He could do. As modern-day disciples, we can sometimes grow comfortable about what He can do and forget that He can do greater and much more.
2) The disciples were in need of a little faith building. As I had previously mentioned, it seems as though Jesus was preparing them for the other side and for life after the cross—a time when He no longer would be with them in body. It was time for them to understand and expect more than what their eyes were seeing.
3) On the other side, Jesus had greater things in store for them. He had purpose, and He did so much more than the disciples ever imagined. He promised it to them.

We will discuss the third answer in the following chapters, but all three reasons find parallels with us today. Sometimes, it takes a storm for God to do His work.

Chapter 4

When Things Don't Make Sense

"And when the disciples saw him walking on the sea, they were troubled, saying, "It is a spirit;" and they cried out for fear."

—Matthew 14:26 (KJV)

As I was reading commentary on this specific passage of scripture, I came across conflicting reports regarding what scholars think the disciples saw. I have always been curious about what crossed their minds One scholar suggests that the reason the disciples and their countrymen believed Jesus was a spirit wasn't solely due to the fact that He was walking on the water, but also because He was in a transfigured state, i.e., glowing. That had not happened before this point. What a sight to behold! How breathtaking it must have been to see the beauty of grace walking amongst chaos. Other scholars state that the disciples were afraid because walking on water was a supernatural event. Jesus was away praying and then, out of nowhere, in the middle of a storm, He appeared. This too was not something the disciples, or anyone else for that matter, had experienced. Because Jesus had been some distance away from them, He seemed to be the last one likely to be there.

It's just like God. though, isn't it—to make His moment of appearing so extraordinary and so spectacular. Thus, even when He does appear among the wind and the waves, we are scared to death because He shows up in a way we never imagined and in which only He could arrive. It causes us to ask a few questions of ourselves and of God.

I've previously touched on these questions, but we will ask them time and time again. Once I was heart- broken, distraught, and confused. I'd thought I had it all figured out, but I found myself stranded, in the middle of my storm without any direction other than to reach the other side. I was angry at God. I did not understand why I had pursued something He seemed to have promised me only to watch it to sink. I was driving home from work and trying to pray, but I had no words. All I had was a few questions. Finally, when I got home, I lay down on the floor of my closet and chose to get real with God for a while. I asked myself these simple questions and suspect all Christians have asked (or will ask) themselves these questions as well:

1) If you promised me this thing, why have I been thrust into this dark, troubling time and this storm? What is the point in all of this?

2) Did I misunderstand you? Am I not as close to you as I thought I was? Don't I know your voice like I once did? Have my desires overtaken your words?

3) God, are you angry at me for some reason? If not, why is the opposite of what I've prayed for happening? Why am I having trouble thinking of the words to speak to you?

4) God, where are you in all of this? Why are you running so late?

There is nothing wrong with going to God when you are broken and desperate. I think He delights in those who are real with Him, and it is in those humble moments of quiet solitude that He speaks the loudest and the clearest.

The moment we see God in the middle of the storm, though, we ask ourselves a fifth question as we are still skeptical and filled with more doubt than fear.

1) God, if—and that's a big *if*— this really is you, then do I not know you like I thought I did? Am I not as close to you as I thought was? I thought I knew you, but why didn't I know you like this?

I'm sure the disciples mentally jotted down their questions. As they stared at Jesus, they didn't recognize Him. They thought He was a spirit! They doubted, worried, and were concerned for their lives. We react in the same way, even after years of a relationship with Him, even after years of God saving us and moving on our behalf. We've seen His blueprints. We've watched Him move, but still we doubt.

Nothing made sense to the disciples, so I'm sure they had questions. They thought Jesus was gone, far away from them.

I imagine John shaking his fists in the air, looking at the sky as the waves splashed on his face, and yelling, "Why, God?! How did we go from miracles and wonders to being stranded in a storm?! What did I ever do to you?"

And perhaps James was grumbling and complaining: "Lord, you promised us the other side, but here we are stuck in this stupid boat. We're going to die!"

I know it seems a little dramatic, but isn't that how we react today? We ask God what we did to deserve this with moans, grumbling, and fear. We act as though He has retaliated against us. But could it be that the situation has nothing to do with what we've expected and everything to do with what He wants to do for us? At the very first sight of trouble, we think God is nowhere to be found, the situation is hopeless, and we're all going to die. The disciples were not much different; they were terrified in the storm.

Still, despite their doubt and their questions, Jesus kept walking forward as the water lapped around His ankles. Here, again, is where many scholars differ in opinion. Some people believe Jesus was walking on water to show that He wouldn't always take them out of the storm, but that He would always wait on the other side for them. Perhaps He wanted to show that He would always go before us. Others believe that Jesus sought to show us that, even in the midst of our storms, He is walking with us. The storms we encounter will turn our entire belief system on its head. Whether good or bad, they will build up our faith.

Could both theories be true? Does it matter that there are so many questions? Does it matter that sometimes, the storms we have to go through and the way Jesus seems to work on our behalf as well as the pace at which He moves don't always make sense? The answer is no. He knows what He is doing. He just wants us to trust Him about the outcome.

I believe all Jesus wanted when He walked on the water was His disciples' attention, and He definitely got it. I believe all He wants in our lives is our attention. He wants us to fix our eyes on Him and trust Him. He wants us to believe in Him even when we do not know He is moving, when we seem to have no reason to trust Him, when He doesn't immediately calm the storm. He wants us to know that when things don't make sense, when we have many questions and little evidence, He is the only answer we need.

He will always see us through to the other side. The question is, will you be like the disciples and turn your attention to Him? When things don't make sense, cling to the only answer that matters—Jesus. In his commentary titled "The New Testament of our Lord and Savior Jesus Christ", Joseph Benson said something very powerful that encouraged me to cling to Jesus. He said, "Even appearances of deliverance sometimes occasion's trouble and perplexity to God's people." Therefore, even when things do not make sense and death seems to be coming your way, God will deliver you from your storm. There is great power in turning your focus on Him.

Chapter 5

Where Is God in All of This?

"And when he had sent the multitudes away, he went up into a mountain apart to pray: and when the evening was come, he was there alone ... And in the fourth watch of the night Jesus went unto them, walking on the sea."

—*Matthew 14:23, 25 (KJV)*

Now, before we move any further in this chapter, I must take you back to a few very important verses. Recall the question I posed in the previous chapter? Where is God, and why does He always seem to be running late? It's easy to lose heart and lose sight of God and the other side when so much is going on around us and we cannot feel Him moving. But I want you to take notice of Jesus's position in Matthew 14:23. He was sitting higher than the storm. Praying. Alone.

Scripture doesn't mention what He was praying about. He could have been weeping about the death of John the Baptist, seeking sympathy from the Father. He might have been praying for strength. But perhaps Jesus was interceding on behalf of His disciples. Perhaps He asked that they would not lose heart and would retain their trust in Him, so they could learn and grow in the midst of the storm and prepare for the other side.

Maybe this storm was the ultimate building ground of faith. Perhaps it was a trial of their faith—to urge them to seek help from

God more earnestly, to show that even when they could not see Jesus, His power was still there. They soon would have to learn that lesson when Jesus died and sent them His spirit. Perhaps this was the experience of faith that ultimately led them to the Holy Spirit that helped them perform miracles and turn the world upside down, and Jesus merely spoke on their behalf while He was praying with the Father. I believe that Jesus was praying to ensure the disciples would be prepared for what He promised on the other side.

While their teeth clattered in fear in the darkness of the early morning, Jesus was high above the storm, preparing to make His presence known. Then He walked ever so gently toward them, as He does in our lives. Certainly, He has done that in my life. The time is desperate. The winds chill us to the bone. We are shaken to our core. Our faith hangs in the balance. Our trust in God and His word is wavering. We are in the darkest and most dangerous part of the storm, and we question our chances for survival: will we ever make it out of this storm and obtain His promise? It is then that God shows up but is often unnoticed. God is moving, and we are unaware. We've asked, where is God in all of this? And the answer is, God is sitting high above the storm, watching over us. He is making provision for us. He is waiting for the perfect time to move, and the perfect time is always His.

That is what's important about Matthew 14:25, "And in the fourth watch of the night Jesus went unto them, walking on the sea." The Jews and Romans in this time period often divided the night into four watches of three hours each. The first one started at 6:00 p.m., the second at 9:00 p.m., the third at 12:00 a.m. and the fourth at 3:00 a.m. Here were the disciples, professional fishermen, exhausted and completely overwhelmed in the middle of the night. It was very dark, and they were distressed and rowing fervently, unable to see where they were going. They had to fight the winds and waves while they stood in a place of hopelessness, in need of prayer and help.

Although the disciples did not see Jesus, He saw them. He saw them struggle. He saw the nose of the boat dip into the water, and the waves crash against His humbled followers. Yet Jesus waited until the darkness of the fourth watch to come to their rescue. He saw that it would ultimately try their faith and patience. The storm did not stop. It didn't quiet or slow down. The disciples, as our fragile, human nature often does, lost hope in deliverance, lost hold of His promises. And then suddenly, Jesus went to them in such a tremendous and unprecedented way—by walking on water, on crashing waves. There He was—running behind according to our schedule but never late according to His.

His appearance and his actions are often unexpected, perhaps when we least expect them, but that is because His ways and His timing are so much better than ours are. He considers us far too important, loves us far too much, and is far too limited by our simple minds; as a result, He refuses to do anything in a normal way. God appears, triumphantly in our storms, in the fourth watch. He is already moving on our behalf as the storm becomes our foundation of faith, because He loves us, and He will always see us through.

How true it is today. As we face our storms, God often lengthens our troubles, and like our hope, He has deferred the time of our deliverance. How often is it that our hope and time of deliverance in healing, restoration, mending or whatever it may be, has been deferred and looked completely hopeless? How long have you been in your storm? Is it the fourth watch yet?

Are you unable to see God or where He is directing you to go? Are things failing to add up or make sense? Do you wonder where He is, and why He is running behind schedule? Have you been there? Are you willing to give up when the storm has gone on too long, it seems too dark, and you believe there is no way God can fulfill His promise?

If so, do not lose heart, because when the situation is extreme, and you think God has forgotten you, i.e., in your darkest hour, He will unexpectedly appear for your relief, rescue and promise. He will come to walk with you. When the darkness is overwhelming, Jesus will walk with you for support and comfort. His eyes constantly watch over you, His hands are ever reaching.

So, where is God in all of this? God is on His way to us. Why is He running behind? Perhaps He isn't. What the disciples saw—and what we often see today—as a delay in God's promise is often due to our impatience and misplaced expectations rather than His failure to keep His word.

God is preparing us for a triumphant victory over our storms, and He will never disappoint. He does exceedingly and abundantly more than we could ever think, ask, or imagine. But what do we do in the meantime?

Chapter 6

In the Meantime

"But straightway Jesus spoke unto them, saying, "Be of good cheer; it is I; be not afraid." And Peter answered him and said, "Lord, if it be thou, bid me come unto thee on the water.""

—Matthew 14:27–28 (KJV)

What will I do in the meantime? That is the question I have asked God more times than my pride will allow me to count. I've been angry, hurt, exhausted, and felt stranded, confused, and without direction. I've grown annoyed and I have felt misled. Once I needed some spiritual advice, and I messaged a mentor of mine, someone I depend on and greatly trust. In my defeated, impatient state of mind, I vented to him through text messages for hours: I was exhausted by the storm, because everything was falling apart, and because I was still waiting for God to move. I told him that I was done with my sister's cancer coming back time and time again. All he did was ask me this question: "what will you do in the meantime?" Nothing could have angered me more. It's the question we hate to ask or to be asked, because then we must fact the fact we cannot fix our own problems. We cannot speed up the process. We cannot solve the puzzle. It's humbling when we realize we do not know what to do.

"What will you do in the meantime?" In my mind, the

question suggested that my mentor didn't care about my problems and was not even worried about me.

I grew very angry, but not because he didn't have answers. I was not even at mad at him. But his words didn't give me any comfort. They didn't encourage me. They left me dejected, and I'd wanted to blame somebody. So I chose not to reply. I walked to my room, threw my phone on the bed, and again found myself crying face down on the floor of my closet. There I was, venting, yelling, only this time it was at God, and I didn't have many words to say. I just cried and complained. The funny thing is, God asked me the same question: "what will you do in the meantime?" I was so angry! I had tried to avoid a question asked by someone godly and very important, and then God asked me the same thing. He was challenging me.

It's funny how He works sometimes. He truly has a great sense of humor. He tries to get our attention, while we run from Him, hoping we can ignore Him. Then He confronts us when we are even more vulnerable and cannot stop Him from speaking to us. He waits until we are alone. In my case, though, I posed the same question to God. I asked Him what I was supposed to do while I was in this chasm between what I believed He had promised me and where I stood. Where was it meant to lead me?

I lay there for what seemed like forever and not a single answer came to me. But I was challenged and driven to find an answer. So I began to do exactly what God had intended: seek Him and His Word. I wrote the question down in my iPad. The answer remained blank for a long time. Only months later did God direct me to Matthew 14 and all of this start coming to me. The answers to life's questions are found in the Bible, including advice for what we are supposed to do in the meantime.

Life seems to be more about the meantime and less about the destination. It is where the most growth, preparation, and spiritual transformation happens. What happens when we are waiting for our promise? What do we do, and how should we prepare for

God's appearance? Could it be that the simplest answer is also the hardest to accept? Sometimes while we are in the midst of our storms and He has not given us more direction, we must simply stay the course.

In verse 27, Jesus gives the first step in handling the problems in the meantime. Just as the disciples see Him and start to panic and worry about what may happen, He gives them the first direction to victory. He says "Be of good cheer; it is I; be not afraid." The Greek word translated as *cheer* means to have courage and comfort. Jesus was telling His disciples, as He tells us, not to be overcome with fear, dread, worry, depression, and disbelief, but rather to have courage, cheer, comfort, and faith. Why? In the process of hour-long setbacks, rowing in the dark, near-death experiences and questions upon questions, why should they be of good cheer? Why does God ask this of us?

The answer is, because He is God. He walks on the water. He loves us too much to drown. He loves us too much to sink. His appearance not only in but on our storm is not by happenstance; it is divine providence. We were created to marvel at His appearance and His presence, to be cheerful—not fearful—when He arrives. It's easy to have good cheer when all is well, but when there is tribulation, where does our cheerfulness go? How fickle is our faith. Being of good cheer isn't based on the absence of trouble; rather it is based on the knowledge that we will overcome, even in the midst of trouble. All Jesus wanted from the disciples was to be noticed as their deliverer, but their eyes, as ours often do, deceived them. So He made His presence known. Only then, when Jesus announced His arrival and their minds were set right and focused on Him, were they were able to walk in faith.

Peter did what we all must do in the meantime. God blesses those who take action. Peter's words should resonate with us: "Lord, if it be thou, bid me come unto thee on the water." When he grasped who was walking on the water—that it was not a spirit or a ghost but the Holy One—he had the faith to ask

Jesus for that same ability. And do you know what happened in the meantime, in the midst of this tumultuous storm? God gave Him that power—not just to walk on water but to walk on and through rising waves and push through heavy winds. Peter was the only man aside from Jesus to walk on water! Why is that? Of everyone in that boat, why Peter? Because he asked. It was that simple. He had the faith to ask and the faith to listen. Jesus said "come," and Peter obeyed!

Peter could have doubted that Jesus had told him to come. He might have thought, *Maybe that was the wind blowing rather than a response from the Lord.* Amid all the noise and danger around him, it would have been easy to not hear or to hear something that wasn't said.

I have always imagined that Peter separated himself from the other disciples and got closer to Jesus before he asked to be able to walk on the water. Although I have no evidence to back it up, could that have been his closet moment? Jesus was alone with Peter in a place where nothing could be misinterpreted or misheard. Peter knew Jesus and His voice well enough to know who was and who wasn't Him. Peter heard and didn't second-guess His direction ... at least, not yet.

Imagine how much we could do. Imagine what our faith and trust in God could accomplish—if we only handled things the way Peter did, if we didn't second-guess what God says us, and if we had enough confidence to make a move. Perhaps we simply need to step out of our boat in faith and take action. Trust and obey. When He says move, we must always move. We must not hesitate, even though we sometimes get comfortable with our aches and pains, even when the storm beyond the boat scares us.

Even though our boats are still dangerous, we've lived in them for so long, we have grown comfortable with the little shelter they provide. But instead we should be walking toward the One who can bring us out and to the things He has promised.

Why don't we do so? Because we are afraid—that we will

sink, the cancer will come back, we'll get hurt or rejected again, the test results won't be good, the marriage will fall apart. Perhaps you're scared your friends will walk out? When obedience to God in the meantime is more important than safety and comfort, it's much more rewarding.

God will not lead us astray. He will not leave us to fend for ourselves. But He definitely will not allow us to stay in our boat either. He is not a God who wants us to grow complacent in our storms. He doesn't want us to just barely make it out. He wants to call us out and to walk with Him. He wants us to have faith in Him—to be in awe of Him, not the storms.

He wants to bless us and fulfill His promises. He wants to get us to the other side. So keep your heart, eyes and mind fixed on Him. Be of good cheer, brother. Be of good cheer, sister. Be obedient to God, for He has overcome the world, and His only desire is to help you grow and fulfill His plans for you. Step out, and make your way to Jesus.

What matters more than anything else in the meantime is that we say to ourselves "This storm will not preoccupy my mind." Sometimes, we may have to be more specific, e.g., "Cancer will not preoccupy my mind." "Fear will not preoccupy my mind." What will it be for you? Write it down. Say it to yourself and pray about it. "_____ will not preoccupy my mind." God will lead you to the other side. Do not let your storm distract you from what God has promised you, and do not let it distract you from Him.

Chapter 7

Staying Afloat in the Storm

"And he said, "Come." And when Peter was come down out of the ship, he walked on the water, to go to Jesus. But when he saw the wind boisterous, he was afraid; and beginning to sink, he cried, saying, "Lord, save me.""

—*Matthew 14:29–30 (KJV)*

What do we do when we begin to sink? That is the exact moment our storm begins to become too much. It's when doubt, fear, and confusion overwhelm us, and we think all of our hope for the other side was for nothing. It's the moment we are ready to accept defeat. But then Jesus stretches forth His hand. So how do we stay afloat in the storm? It's quite the important question to ask, and it's important to figure out. Peter definitely could have used the answers here once he bravely stepped onto the water in obedience to Jesus. Because after he'd seen Jesus, obeyed Him, and walked on the water, he was distracted by the dangers of his act of obedience. He became frightened by what this storm could do.

How do we stay afloat in the storm? To answer that question to our fullest ability, we must first figure out what caused Peter to sink. From my perspective, I'd say doubt caused him to sink. In the next verse, Jesus asks him "Why are you of so little faith?" He could have asked, "Did I not tell you to come? Am I not standing right beside you? And you're still afraid, Peter? You are sheltered when I am with you, and safe from all harm."

We respond to God the same way. We go to Him and ask things of Him as though we have faith. Then the moment God tells us to do something and we want to obey, things get scary. The opposite of faith is either complacency or doubt. We grow content where we are, even if it's hard or uncomfortable. So we stay there—in our boats, undetermined and unhappy. But at least we are content and comfortable with our problems instead of stepping out and risking getting wet.

Often though, our complacency is rooted in doubt and fear. Doubt that we will reach the other side. Doubt that we can survive the storm. Doubt that we can make it out alive. Doubt that God will calm the storm when He shows up or that He will show up at all. Fear that His presence will not stop bad things from happening again. Sometimes, we doubt that He cares. But He is in the storm with us, and He does care. We just grow too used to the storm to realize He wants to do good for us. My point is the question: "Why are we sinking in our problems now when we thought we'd conquered them yesterday?"

It is the same reason Peter walks on water before he begins to sink. Our problems are bigger now, because our faith is smaller. God can save you from the flood. But you will sink anyway, because you are weighed down by doubt about potential outcomes that may not even happen and no longer cling to faith in Christ Jesus. In the next few chapters, we will talk about how Jesus stretched forth His hand to Peter. I'll probably mention this again, but it's important to know and remember: Jesus stretches forth His hand not only so we can walk on water but so that we can also overcome the water. It wasn't that Peter didn't have faith. It was that he lost it when he started to think about the potential outcomes of his decision.

For example, he expects to drown, even though there is no sign that he is sinking. In fact, the complete opposite could be said. It looks like Jesus was helping him through an impossible situation. He allows Peter to walk on water and takes him out of the storm, which was something no one had ever experienced. It is Peter's doubt and fear of a potentially bad outcome that changes what could have been accomplished through Jesus Christ. Think about the things Jesus does to get Peter here:

He shows up, let's Peter know He is there, and then He calls on Peter to make a move. Before all of this, Jesus already had promised the other side to him. He stacks everything in Peter's favor—including giving him the power to walk on the water—without removing the storm.

Peter didn't sink because of the waves or the winds. He sunk because He had doubt. He ignored what Jesus said to do when things get scary. We are exactly the same. We're stranded in the storm until God appears. Time after time and reason after reason, He gives us an incentive to obey and trust Him. Even if everything isn't perfectly clear, we can step back and evaluate what He has done. In addition, we should be able to take solace in the fact that He is moving. And we do obey. We do move, but the moment we realize the unlikelihood of what He is speaking, we start to open our eyes to the dangers of it. We overthink and look too far into all the potential outcomes.

The thing He gave us the power to overcome and defeat, the thing He wanted us to work through, and the thing He is using to build our faith is the thing defeats us again. We ignore the breadcrumbs He uses to give us hope, power, and strength, and we see what should have been a blessing as a reason to be scared. Imagine if Peter never took his eyes away from God, if he never had doubt. He probably could have walked to the other side of the Sea of Galilee.

You don't want to sink, you say? Can I encourage you not to lose heart, not to doubt? Can I ask you to worry a little less and trust a little more, to stay focused on the Lord and have hope? I understand this is easier said than done. You see, hope is not a possibility or potential. Hope is the belief that something will eventually happen while trusting in the fact that God works for our good.

What we go through may not always be good to us, but it's always good for us. Storms may cut and bruise us. They will give us scars. They will make us uncomfortable and soaking wet. They may have us shaking in our boots, terrified. They will purge us of all our weaknesses and it will hurt. But we can overcome. We can walk upon our storms. If we do not want to sink, we must let the Lord move on our behalf. We must stop trying and start trusting in Him because *all* things work together for our good.

When we let Him move, God will do for us what Jesus Christ did for Peter. He will show up. He will make Himself known. He will tell us what to do. He will give us the power to walk through our storms, and He will walk with us. Of course, there will be those times before He shows up, when we aren't sure what to do, where to go, or even why we should be of good cheer and take courage in God's promises. At times, we will wonder why we need to have faith before God does any of those things.

There's an old children's song that offers the perfect steps to staying afloat: read your Bible, and pray every day. That is wonderful advice. When God has not yet appeared in the storm, when He is on his way to His glorious appearance, but not yet where we are, we can find peace in His Word. The Bible doesn't change; it doesn't grow ineffective with time, and the Bible is truth. His Word even says in Psalms 119:105, "Thy word is a lamp unto my feet and a light unto my path." While we look for guidance or direction and wonder where to go, He will often lead us through His Word. We must be obedient and sensitive to it for His Word does not return void.

At times, we will cry out to Him for help, and Jesus will delay His response. That is not a reason for us to stop speaking to Him. In fact, it is then that we must pursue Him even more, yearn for Him more abundantly. That is what He desires from us. Relationships and communication are built; from them come strength and growth. There is power in prayer and power in the one who is on the other side of our prayers. Although it may seem that He is nowhere to be found, He is never so far that His ears cannot hear our voices.

Another important thing that keeps us from sinking is the church—not just the building, but the fellowship. You will find comfort in like-minded, faithful people. Often, the first thing people want to do when adversity strikes is cut themselves off from their church, when that is the last thing they should do. It is of great value to keep close those who encourage you in Christ. They will worship with you and remind you about His infallible Word when distractions and storms steer your mind in other directions. I can tell you with assurance that the body of Christ (the church) can heal you. When my sister had just passed away from cancer and my family was hurting and grieving, it was hard not to lose faith and heart. It was hard to face a line of people hugging us and crying on our shoulders. Many people said we were strong as a family, but the truth is, we had the body of Christ behind us. Church members gave us words of encouragement, loved us, and built up our faith. The storm didn't get any easier or lighter, but the body of Christ helped carry the load. There truly is great power in numbers. The first thing I wanted to do after everything had settled is the very same thing that can help us stay afloat in the storm: to go back to church and the people who walked with us. I wanted to be with the people who would encourage us to fight, not duck our heads and run.

The Lord desires and creates strong communion with and between His people for a reason—that we may stay strong in our faith and not weighed down by doubt and fear. In the midst of two or three Christians, He is there. Let us lift each other up in our storms.

Of course, none of this is possible and none of it matters unless we trust God enough to believe He will protect us during the storms. We must believe His words and not second-guess them. The power to overcome is at our fingertips. But we cannot take our eyes off of Jesus Christ. We cannot lose faith and hope in Him. If He tells us to do something that can save us, we must be obedient and do it. It not only may lead us out of the storm, it may take us to what He promised us, to what He has written on our hearts.

A final point I would like to touch on in this chapter is that when Jesus told Peter to come out of the boat, it took courage on Peter's part, which came from his faith that he could do something that he'd thought couldn't be done. What step has God asked you to take in a situation that looks and feels hopeless? Is it to apologize to someone and make things right, to give more in the offering, to take action and make a move, to drive until He says stop? Is He calling you into the unknown? What is He asking you to do, and in which direction is He asking you to move?

It is probably not just scary but downright terrifying. It probably looks unlikely. It may seem that the outcome can only end badly. The best advice—beyond reading and studying your Bible, praying every day, and going to church— is to listen when God says "go" or "do." When you think it can't be done, must fix your eyes on Him, and follow His lead. He won't leave you to drown. He will not leave you without any encouragement. He will not leave you at all. Obey Him, every word and in every way. Believe in Him and not in what your storms tell you.

It is so easy to grow disheartened and become just like Peter did when he took his eyes off Jesus and began to sink. We've seen what the waters have done before, the troubles our misunderstandings, mistakes, and failures have caused. We've seen the pain that stepping out has caused before, and yet He tells us to walk on the water again? It's scary, but it's exactly where God wants us. It may seem that God is doing this for His amusement and to our detriment. It may seem that He is playing some terrible game, but that is not further from the truth. Stay focused on the

Lord. Believe in Him. Look beyond the dangerous, ugly storm. Do not put more faith in your storm than you do in Him. Look into the fullness of His wonderful face, and do not allow your circumstances to tell you He doesn't care, because that is not at all who He is. Trust and keep your eyes on who God is.

Chapter 8

Who God Is

This may seem like a detour, but I believe it's important to figure out the answer to this question before we continue: who is God? Clearly, I don't have a scripture for this chapter. It's not because there isn't one, but because all throughout the Bible, God reveals Himself to His people, often in deeply personal ways. He appeared in the middle of the fiery furnace to Shadrach, Meshach, and Abednego. He appeared to Elijah in the cave—not as a mighty wind, earthquake, or fire, but as a still small voice. Jesus appeared to Peter on the water, in the midst of a storm. In all three occurrences, people were in the midst of trials, in desperate and seemingly hopeless situations. The end seemed so real to them.

Shadrach, Meshach, and Abednego should have lost their lives in the fire. Elijah feared for his life in the cave. Peter thought he was drowning. Yet God was personal enough to be what they needed at different times.

There are so many more stories like these, and if you study the Bible long enough, you'll find your own answers. There is so much more to God that sometimes we must take a personal journey with Him to figure it out. We often are sent on this journey in the midst of our storms or our trial. It's mentally tasking, exhausting, and sometimes disheartening. Often these are our lowest moments.

But out of the fire comes strength and gold. Out of the water comes the ability to overcome. Out of the cave comes the calmness of God. As I've mentioned before, our storms aren't always good to us, but they are always good for us, and these are prime examples. They draw us closer to God and Him closer to us. They strengthen us. They bring forth wisdom. They purge us of our impurities and prepare us for His promise. They build our relationship with Him, and we may not even know it during the storm, but we will always see it on the other side.

I'd like to share with you a part of my journey to find out who God is. It was a dark time, and I was in the middle of the roughest patch of my life. I was mentally and spiritually drained. I believed God had promised me something, and I stepped out in faith—only to watch my faith crumble in my hands and my entire belief system turn upside down.

Not only was what I thought He'd promised me unfulfilled, but everything else that had been going good seemed to be falling away. My sister's cancer was the worst it had ever been. My family, fearful of cancer, was struggling and were always isolated from each other. My friendships were shattered and people seemed to leave every time I turned around. My heart was hurting. I was confused and disheartened.

I was angry at God. Just like Peter, Shadrach, Meshach, and Abednego, and Elijah, I was at my wit's end, at my own end. In my situation, however, it seemed my storm had conquered me. I certainly had accepted defeat. All I thought I knew about God seemed uncertain. I didn't know how to pray anymore. I thought my storm would never end, and I was ready to embrace the wind and waves. I thought I deserved this storm and that I had created it. I also struggled with being obedient to God. I fled from the words He spoke to my heart. I'd literally feel Him prick my heart and would cover my ears with my hands and deny that He was speaking to me.

During one our camp meetings I had felt Him dealing with me, urging me to make things right with someone who was dear to me, but I was terrified of the outcome. I didn't want to hurt or hurt anyone else, and I expected that my obedience to His word would cause hurt, because everything else seemed to do so. The weight was heavy on my shoulders, and I kept making up new excuses on why I shouldn't do what I knew I needed to do. In my prayers, I said, "I'll make things right once they make things right." I kept giving God an ultimatum for my obedience, as I tried to make absolutely sure it was Him. I had grown tired of faking my smile and wrestling with God over it. All of that, accompanied with my storm, caused me to second-guess everything God had said to me and all that I thought He was.

Every message had been spoken directly to me, yet my mind wandered all over the place. I ignored every moment of God trying to get my attention. Finally on Thursday morning of that week, God sent someone, a preacher, to encourage and help me. That is where this question was born: who is God?

The preacher's message was directed at me and my situation. He spoke about God pulling things out of the scrapyard that looked like hopeless trash and about restoration. Still, I tried with all my might, as I was at the altar weeping, to ignore what God was saying. I didn't know what to say or what to listen to. Then I said the first words that came to my mind. I said, "Who are you, God? I thought I knew you. I thought I had a relationship with you, but who are you? Do you even love me?" As I was at the altar on this camp ground, I realized I was so mad at God, I didn't even know I was mad at Him.

It was then that I felt a hand press on my back, and another mentor of mine spoke to me. This man from my church leaned into my chest and told me as we were praying that I was struggling because I needed to come to peace with whom God is. That was my turning point in my storm. God used a willing vessel, after I ignored everything else. He met me in my fire. He met me in my raging waters. He called me out of my cave and, when I ignored Him time and time again, He met me in a personal, intimate moment. There I was. This was my opportunity to know Him at the most deep, intimate, and personal level in my life. This was my opportunity to build a relationship with Him. In the midst of my prayer, I began to understand and realize what His attributes are. God is powerful. He is a God of restoration. He is hope. He is joy. He is peace. He is our comfort.

But these things are not even what God is. All of those things are great, and they are a part of what and who He is, but He isn't that! Some say He is wrath, and some say He is love, and they too are parts of who He is, but that is also wrong. The fact is, God is all of these things, but He is so much more than that. There is not enough depth in the seas and there are not enough heights to adequately describe all that He is, because He cannot be put in a box. The moment we think we have Him figured out, the moment we think we have His ways figured out, He meets our needs a different, unique, and personal way. The best way I can put it is that God is simply faithful in ways we will never fully understand.

Why did Jesus reach down for Peter in the water, even after Peter was full of fear and lacked faith? He's faithful. Why did God appear in the middle of fire? He's faithful. Why did He whisper to Elijah in a still small voice? He's faithful. Why did He send His only begotten Son to reach for us? He's faithful. Why does He speak to us and try to get our attention in the middle of our messes and our obedience? He's faithful. And why does God pull for us through the midst of our storms?! He loves us, and He is faithful.

I must clarify. In the middle of all of this, I realized that yes, God is good, and yes, God is love. He is caring and faithful. But He is also righteous, and He is just. Therefore, He will purge you of all the things that are not pure in your life. He will get you to the end of yourself—that means your timing and your way as He rids you of impatience, pride, fear, and doubt. He is too faithful to keep you as you are. He knows you for where you are going to be, not for where you currently are. He will do what it takes to get you there.

Even when He tries to speak and our doubts speak louder, He will get our attention. He's faithful. When it seems that we have all the right questions but never enough answers and our faith fits in the palm of our hands, God is trying to show us that a little faith can rearrange landscapes and that faith comes by His Word. He is trying to show us that before we doubt Him, we must doubt our doubts. The truth is that we know His truth. We know He is in the middle of our storms and that there is a reason to hold on. He is the author and finisher of our faith, and we know to whom we belong.

Like Peter and like me at that altar, when it seems like we are drowning in the sea of our questions, God longs for us to just know that He is there and that He is faithful. It's true. He is all of this, and when I try to describe Him, I can only speak of these things. Yet He is even more than that. God is God, and He is more than enough. When I wonder how or why He loves me, I can only think that He loves me because He loves me. There is no explanation. He shouldn't love me. He shouldn't be all that He is for me. From the very beginning, we have let Him down, and we have paid the price every time, because He is just. Yet He never leaves us without extending a hand because He too is love. He is unexplainable, but God is God and that is more than enough. Imagine what He can do when we are obedient to Him. Imagine what He will do if we hold on to Him. He will make a way out, and He will work.

Work He certainly did. You see, as I prayed and prayed for God to restore my friendship during that camp meeting and take me out of the storm, I allowed my fear to get in the way. I feared God wasn't speaking to the others the way He was speaking to me. I allowed impatience to get in the way. I didn't have the faith in God I should have had, so I placed my stipulations and my timeframe on Him. I acted as though I knew better than He did. I told God to send them my way by the end of the week, or I was done. And then even as He was doing everything to get me to a place where He could work it out, I allowed disobedience to get in the way. I saw the negatives and I refused to make the move He was telling me to make. A day later than I expected, after I finally chose to make a move, God restored what had been broken for so long. He did work that has lasted to this day and is still healed. He healed things that could have been healed much earlier had I been obedient. As time went on, I had found out that God had spoken to the other person about doing the exact same thing. We just got in the way. My point is that sometimes His delay in fulfilling His promises and taking us out of our storms is directly caused by our failure to obey.

We should not find ourselves in the place I found myself— held back by doubt, worry, fear, pride, too many questions and not enough answers. We need to find ourselves in a deeper place with God. We need to find Him in our fire, our cave, and our stormy waters. And when we wonder where He is and who He is, we will know that He is faithful, even when it looks unlikely. He is sovereign, but beyond that, God is ever moving.

He is working when we cannot see and when we struggle to obey. He is our whisperer when we need a calming voice; He is our hand when we are sinking. He is fire all-consuming, and He is a restorer and a direction giver when we are obedient. He is who He is when we don't deserve it and when it seems too good to be true. He is grace. Grace has a face, and grace has a name, and it is Jesus.

Trust who God is, and get to know Him, because He is the one reaching for you in the middle of the storm. It will take all the faith you can muster to reach out and cling to Him.

Chapter 9

What Is the Point in Holding On?

"And immediately Jesus stretched forth his hand, and caught him, and said unto him, "O thou of little faith, wherefore didst thou doubt?" And when they were come into the ship, the wind ceased."

—*Matthew 14:31–32 (KJV)*

After all this time, there Peter was. His faith battled his doubt. His fleshly fear seemed to yell louder than God's words. His perspective based on fear argued God's viewpoint of faith, and there He was with enough courage and faith to obey God's direction to walk on the water, and He had failed miserably! He had completely and utterly failed!

Imagine the scene. Jesus says "Come" and Peter steps over the side of the boat and into the dangerous waters. The waves were over his head; the winds were strong enough to blow him away. The disciples were probably speechless as they hung on to the sides of the boat. They were witnessing something that they had never seen before and were too afraid to do what Peter was attempting. But there he was walking on the water, unharmed and unfazed.

Then, just as quickly as he stepped out of the water, focused on Jesus, Peter looked around, and human nature set in. He realized how unlikely his situation was. He looked at the towering waves and the rocking boat as his eyes hopped around from left to right. Peter's faith started to fleet. He realized that this was not the way things go. It was outside the realm of possibilities.

Humans didn't walk on water, most certainly not when the storms are raging. Right there—that is where it began. Peter's doubt, his fear, and his worry changed everything in a moment's time. Not only did he stop walking on the water, not only did he stumble and probably belly flop, smashing face first into the water, he began to sink!

I doubt it was a graceful fall. It was probably a struggle. He'd taken a step of faith, hoping to be rescued from his storm. He was unsure of the outcome and worried that he had not heard Jesus correctly. None of it made sense. None of it seemed likely. It went against all logic. By faith he was simply obedient, but in his obedience, he still stumbled. He still messed up. How confusing this must have been to Peter.

He got into the boat as Jesus told him to do, but the storm seemed to never end, and hope and faith faded away. Just when he and the other disciples believed Jesus had forgotten about them, Jesus showed up and spoke to them. Surely he believed that Jesus's words would lead him not into greater danger, but out of it. Surely, Peter thought that obedience to His word would bring forth deliverance and a blessing, perhaps even an end to this storm. But Peter sank!

Isn't that how it always seems to go in our lives? Our storms last far longer than we desire. They go on longer than we ever think they should. That crumbling marriage that God urged you to restore is not only still in turmoil, things have grown worse. The bottom has fallen out in other areas of your life. The healings you have been praying for seem to have fallen on deaf ears. Your relationships are still not mended although you've stepped out in faith. Instead you are sinking, the winds are blowing harder, and the waters are rising.

Due to the time that has passed and our perspective of the destruction around us, we doubt He will restore anything. We doubt He will move, and as a result, we not only fall, we collapse. I've absolutely been there and, beyond the shadow of a doubt, it was the hardest time of my life. Like the disciples, I reluctantly stepped into the boat to charter a brand new territory. I had to overcome worry and fear and profess a whole lot of prayer and a little faith, but I stepped in the boat in pursuit of what I felt God had told me to seek out.

It was a journey filled with worry and thrills, tears and laughter, jitters and butterflies. Everything was new, and I was experiencing it for the first time, pursuing what I felt God had promised me. Not only did that thing fall apart in my life, but everything else seemed to as well. It looked like a hopeless situation, a life-shattering storm of irreparable measure. I was most definitely sinking.

Again, I asked God a question. I imagine Peter had a similar thought and that we have all wondered the same thing: *God, what is the point in holding on?*

I stood there, speaking to God, tearing my heart open to Him. I said, "What is the point in holding on? I thought you promised me this, but I'm not seeing any results. Nothing is going at all the way I imagined it would or according to my plan. I don't see an end to this. Why should I cling to you and your words? Wouldn't it be easier to just let it go and move on? Is it even worth holding on to now?"

It was an overwhelming moment, and I imagine it was for Peter too in the middle of the waters, in the dark of the night, feeling alone, embarrassed, ashamed, sinking. Certainly, he thought what he'd heard was a mistake. He was mentally coming apart at the seams. He was sinking deeper and deeper into the waters, which covered his body. All the disciples, Peter included, expected his demise. But the story doesn't end there. Peter had a hold of something in his spirit to which we must all grasp hold. As Peter was sinking, he yelled out to Jesus to save him, and immediately, Jesus stretched forth his hand.

Yes, Peter got scared. Yes, he lost faith. But it seems to me that—though he lost faith in his ability to walk on the water, to stop the storm, to get to the other side, to save himself and the disciples—he didn't lose faith in the ability of Jesus. There is nothing more vital to our lives and to overcoming our storms than trusting God's ability. How many times has He shown Himself to be faithful?

Peter cried out to Him, and Jesus responded with a resounding answer. He stretched forth His hand and caught Peter. This was not a high-five moment. Peter and Jesus didn't high-five each other. They didn't laugh and joke about it. They didn't make up some special handshake. I believe Peter held on in that moment. Freezing, shaking, and scared, he held on, and he let Jesus resolve the issue.

When Jesus first appeared to Peter and even after Peter obeyed Him, there was still a delay before the storm grew calm and Jesus did what He said He would do. The circumstances had not yet changed. But it was after the flailing Peter yelled out for help, and Jesus stretched forth His hand and carried him back to the boat, that everything changed. The storm became calm, the winds ceased, and the waves collapsed under His power.

So it is in our lives. I've mentioned it before, but it's vital to say it again. The calm after the story and the fulfillment of His promises sometimes are delayed even after He appears and we faithfully obey His directions. It's discouraging, it's heartbreaking and it's easy to feel weighed down as we are sinking—as if He's changed His mind or our prayers have angered Him. It's easy to feel like His promises won't come to pass when the opposite seems to be happening. But a delay in His promises is not a denial of His promises.

Could the storms we all face in our lives—the ones that take place before our promises are fulfilled, the ones that lie between us and the other side, the ones that seem to cause our entire lives to fall apart and grow worse—occur simply to exchange unnecessary things for what we will need when we reach the other side? Could the storms be part of our preparation? I believe this is the most likely reason.

It is by His most godly counsel that He renders us capable of receiving His gifts and His works. It's just rare that it occurs on our schedule, for His ways are not our ways and His thoughts are not our thoughts. He gives in ways that we usually don't expect and that cause our faith to waver and in timeframes that do not seem to make sense. There in lies the reason we should hold on.

In that chasm between what we feel God has promised us, where we are and where we are meant to go, we often ask ourselves, what is the point in holding on? This is particularly the case when it seems like we should do the complete opposite, when the complete opposite of what we've prayed for has happened, when nothing makes sense, when everything is bleak, when the delay in His appearance has gone on until the fourth watch. The fact is we hold on because miracles happen on both sides of the storm! Miracles happen in the middle of the storm if we cling to the Rock! Miracles happen when God calls us closer to Him, even when we mess up.

Let me tell you, friend. God does things from one shore to the next and things in-between, and He doesn't ever change! On the other side of your storm, beyond what we can't see, He will fulfill what He has promised. He accomplishes what He said He would accomplish, and He doesn't ever lie. God overcomes what we could never overcome, because He is all powerful, He spoke the world into existence, and He has overcome the world.

We hold on because God is faithful and miracles happen! God is healing, deliverance from depression, restoration in relationships, heart mending. God is good, and He is reaching out to you. Cling to Him.

Hold on tight. He will carry you, when you can't stand, back into your boat, to take you to the other side. He's still speaking promises to you. Hold on to His word, even when they don't look likely, because God keeps His word, and He will never forsake you. Watch as He brings it all to pass in ways you never imagined, in times you never thought, in curious cases that don't seem to add up.

Even in our failures, He is faithful, and He will always move. Often when we have removed all the likelihood of that promise to be fulfilled as our faith and hope are on their last life line, when we have accepted the sinking position we are in, God moves on our behalf. Rarely is it a moment sooner, because it is then that we are at the end of ourselves, and Jesus is ready to step in, reach out, and finally do what He said He would do. It is simply a matter of us holding on to Him.

Chapter 10

Worshipping Wet

"Then they that were in the ship came and worshipped him, saying, "Of a truth thou art the Son of God.""

—*Matthew 14:33 (KJV)*

As we read this scripture and imagine Peter going under, flailing his hands and gasping for breath, we are always quick to point our fingers at him, as if he lacked faith. However, we neglect the fact that he knew his source of strength. Peter was on the brink of drowning and at his wit's end. He didn't know what to do, yet he knew he could call on Jesus. How embarrassing that must have been for poor Peter.

Imagine the scene. The storm is raging; the disciples have exerted all of their energy to keep their boat above water, their voices are growing hoarse from yelling over sounds of crashing water and the howling, whistling winds. No doubt they are frustrated, and tempers boil over. John and James probably bark out orders at their friends. Thomas cowers in the back of the boat, his knees against his chest, cradling in his arms. Terrified or freezing, he rocks back and forth. And here is Peter. He fixes his eyes on Jesus as he wobbles to the side of the boat.

James yells at Peter, telling him to gather his bearings and get back to his post. There is so much going on at this moment, but it doesn't distract Simon Peter from his goal. He keeps walking forward, scraping his arms against the side of the boat, and slipping on the wooden floors. He is determined to get to Jesus and to walk on the water.

Peter knows Jesus. He has walked with Him for so long, and now he sees Jesus walking on water. Peter does what the Son of God is doing, the only person to accomplish such a feat. He steps out in faith, walking on water like no man before him. For once in his life, he finally follows through, and still Peter fails.

None of the other disciples can muster enough faith to do what Peter does—not John, the one whom Jesus loves; not John's fiery brother, James, or doubting Thomas, who definitely will not step foot in the water. It is Simon Peter—the one who always speaks first and thinks later, who is impulsive and makes irrational decisions, who often boasts and then fails to follow through. This is the man who soon would claim he would die for Jesus but then deny Him three times due to fear of persecution. Peter has asked Jesus to let him do a dangerous and impossible thing, i.e., to tread the waters. But he seems to have gotten in too deep, and he's sinking.

I imagine that Peter's personality occasionally clashed with the personalities of the other disciples. He was always talking a big game, walking with his head held high. Thomas probably grumbled complaints about Peter's claims and pride. The sons of thunder never shied away from confrontation and opinion. Perhaps they even wanted to see their friend humbled at times. I often wonder if Jesus Himself rolled His eyes at Peter from time to time. He knew good and well all the things at which Peter would fail. He knew Peter was not yet in a place to lead or even speak confidently to others.

If you take all of this into context, you can almost envision Jesus and the disciples mocking Peter as he begins to sink. Perhaps Jesus throws His hands in the air in dismay and disbelief as he looks at Peter gasping for air. As He reaches toward him, maybe He yells, "Thou fool! You thought you could walk on water like me? You are soaking wet and sinking. Grab my hand, and let's head back to the boat."

Finally, Jesus enters the boat, and the storm ceases. The waves stop raging, the winds are no longer blowing, and there are no words to adequately describe Jesus or this moment. For the first time in hours, there is silence—the perfect opportunity for the disciples to mock Peter. The disciples gather around him as he stands in the boat, dripping from head to toe, drenched in his own undoing.

"Peter, are you all right?" Matthew asks, as Peter wrings the water out of his shirt and exchanges it for a new one. "What did you expect would happen, Simon? You're Simon Peter, not Jesus Christ."

The disciples take him to where Thomas is sitting and clear a space where he can sit down in the back of the boat. Thomas grabs a couple blankets and says, "This is awkward, but you almost had it, Peter. You got further than I could ever get, but I can't say I didn't see this one coming." James or John flicks his nose and says, "See? I told you to keep rowing. You sank because you wouldn't listen to us."

The beauty in this story is that it is not what happened. None of these outcomes took place. The disciples didn't laugh and mock Peter. They didn't kick him when he was down. They didn't document this story and record it in history for their amusement and Peter's humiliation. In fact, they did the complete opposite, and it wasn't even about Peter.

The scripture says that the winds had ceased, and Jesus and Peter entered the boat. Not just Peter, but all of the disciples gathered around and worshipped Jesus. They enjoyed being in His presence and saw who He really was. After all of those sleepless hours away from Jesus, they found rest in Him. After all the chaos, they found out He was the calm. After all the fear and worry, they found peace. After all the doubt, they found hope. Facing death, they found life in the unlikeliest of ways.

They were soaking wet. Simon Peter had failed. They had been in a seemingly pointless storm all night. It was dark. Jesus seemed to be late. They hadn't reached the other side, and they still worshipped Jesus soaking wet! No one noticed Peter's misery. Peter didn't go off in the corner, regretting his actions. The disciples didn't think about how cold they were as the chilly morning breeze brushed against their drenched bodies.

They fell in love with Jesus all over again. The storm didn't matter. Their uncomfortable situation didn't matter. The other side didn't even matter. Jesus had them, and they most certainly had Jesus. Unlike the other storm where Jesus just stopped the wind and waves, they didn't question Jesus. They didn't ask themselves *What sort of man is this, that even the winds and waves obey Him?* They knew, and they certainly acknowledged, who He was: "Surely this is the Son of God."

This is the moment the disciples realized that Jesus is greater than the storm, not just in power but in relevance. That is what this is all about—God restoring and building their hope and relationship with Him. And this is where the application comes in, because some of us are the disciples. We're too focused on surviving the storms, trying to muscle through on our own, yelling at those who brave the side of the boat and attempt to walk in places we would never consider. Some of us are too scared to risk the dangers of obedience and faith as we cower as far away from the storm as possible. We are too reluctant to mess up or embarrass ourselves. Some of us are the finger pointing, judgmental mockers.

But many of us are Peter. We are tired of neither being nor obtaining what we should. We are growing anxious for God's promises and are irritated by our storms. We are trying to fix our eyes on Jesus and are fighting the rocking boat to get to Him. We are risking injury to get ourselves closer to the One who conquers the storms and is in love with us. But the moment we get there, we sink in our doubt. We are terrified, afraid our obedience was a mistake, because it didn't seem change anything. In fact, we seem to be in more danger as we began to sink. But we should thank God for that storm and that sinking, because our sinking will become our closest walk with God as He carries us. It is there that He will fulfill His promises.

But before any of that can happen, we will have to worship wet—just like the disciples did when they were uncomfortable and could have talked about Peter's failures. They worshipped because they were in awe of what God did during the storm. They had expectations about the other side, but their focus was on Him. They fully trusted Him.

It's not always going to be pretty, and it's not always going to peaceful, but we will have to worship wet. We will have to go to church wet, pray wet, read and study our Bibles wet. It will be hard at times. It will be uncomfortable at times. We will not want to do it at times, but my God, we're going to have to worship wet!

We will have to glorify Him when it's hard for us to do. In the midst of sleepless nights, anger-filled thoughts, and broken hearts; when we wonder where He is, why we hurt, why we sink, why our prayers seem to go unanswered or even unheard, why His promises seem delayed, and what we've done wrong—we will have to worship Him for all that He is.

Who is God to you? Is He the One who carries you after you sink, loves you even when you question His ways and doubt His direction, calms your storms and rides with you to the other side? He is the God that is the same yesterday, today, and forever. He is the same God in Matthew 22 as He is today, and He is certainly worthy of your worship all the way to the other side of your storm. Worship, in fact, will get you there.

Chapter 11

The Other Side

"And when they were gone over, they came into the land of Gennesaret. And when the men of that place had knowledge of him, they sent out into all that country round about, and brought unto him all that were diseased; And besought him that they might only touch the hem of his garment: and as many as touched were made perfectly whole."

—*Matthew 14:34–36 (KJV)*

The disciples made it. They reached their destination. After all the questions, worry, fear and doubt, gallons upon gallons of water, darkness, dangers of the storm—after staring death in the face and waiting for Jesus—at last, they had reached the other side. They had arrived on dry land. Rest from their sleepless night was within their grasp!

That's often how it is for us. The other side is meant to be a blessing, but sometimes when we first arrive, we have time to rest as we stand with confidence in God that He has or will fulfill His promise. I wonder how long it took for them to realize they had arrived. Was it immediately? Did they worship so deeply, so passionately, and so purposefully that they lost focus of their position and their destination?

I imagine Jesus first caught their attention as he motioned toward the side of the boat and stepped onto shore. Perhaps He was followed by the stumbling disciples, whose feet had not quite recovered from a long night of rocking. Maybe as they carefully climbed out of the boat and onto dry land, the disciples, still drenched in water, looked around and realized there was no immediate change. There was no instant blessing. This shore was no different than the last one.

I'm curious; did they get a dose of "what's the use," as human nature set in once again and they wondered why they were there. The Bible doesn't say they asked Jesus these questions, but I often have wondered. Did they look around to see what was on this side? Did they wonder if it was worth it and what would happen now that the storm was over? Did they think about what would do once their lives settled down after all the chaos and the pandemonium they had faced? Perhaps as worry and doubt began to fade, wonder and expectancy took up residence.

Does this sound familiar to you? You've endured your greatest hardships and overcome the biggest of storms in your life. You've tried your best to overcome whatever life has thrown your way as it has rocked you back and forth with all its might. You've tried all you know to do and stumbled in the process, because you trusted in God's promises and believed He would bring forth great things beyond the storm. Then you discover that God's love and His power are stronger, and you finally make it to the other side.

However, the moment of your arrival is strained by your own questions. The biggest question is often, what's on the other side? With our simplistic minds, we always wonder what awaits us. There is no shame in this. It's in our nature to anticipate and long for great things. It's in our nature to wonder. But it is our duty, as Paul said in I Corinthians 15:31 to "die daily" to our flesh and our human nature.

When our flesh wants to cry out and demand answers, our spirit is called to quietly trust His Word and let Him lead. When our eyes see nothing but wasted time and we see nothing that makes our pain and time in storms worthwhile, we must know there is more than we perceive and that God looks beyond the shore.

When things don't add up to us, they do to Him, because God has planned and ordained our lives, up to this very moment. He knows our problems before they ever present themselves. He has the answers before we know the questions. And He makes a way out before we ever find ourselves in the storm.

Sometimes, we want to see what's on the other side, usually before we get there. We always want to know what we're getting into, but God rarely shows us until He's tested us and prepared us for it. He purges us of all we are, and His molding will bring forth His miracles and His promises. And when we are ready, God will show us His blessings. He will reveal to us what awaits and He will most definitely begin to work. The truth is, God is faithful, and He is not a settling God, so He will never cause His people to settle for less than what He has. When God moves, it is and always will be overwhelming. The other side is exactly when He proves that His ways are higher than our ways and just how powerful He truly is.

The other side may not look like much when our feet are still in the waters of our storms and we have not yet stepped forward. Some of us have grown so accustomed to the toils, snares and dangers of storms, and have found such comfort in the boat, that it's become all we know, and the other side may seem underwhelming at first. It's easy to grow discouraged during transitional moments.

After the storm has ended and we rest upon the shore, we immediately expect God's divine intervention in our broken marriages; we expect instant healing and for God to wipe cancer clean from our bodies or from our loved ones. We long for God to speak to our unsaved loved ones and transform them into Bible-believing Christians. We expect Him to put our broken relationships back together. We long for that perfect job to fall into our laps, the door to full-time ministry to open up, for the backslider to slide back into God's fold, and for Him to bring His perfect will into our lives.

Rarely do we ever move away from the shore. We wait for God to move, but He waits for us to stop wading in the waters of our past and start moving into the future of the other side. That is when He will moves, and good Lord, it will be greater than we ever imagined.

I confess I've stood on the shore in doubt and wonder—afraid to move in fear of being let down, worried that things will stay bad or get bad again, more scared of the unknown than hopeful of God's blessings. It gets hard to move. I think, if we're honest with ourselves, we grow a little too cautious, which stops us from walking on.

Our lack of blind faith keeps us on that shore, but faith is action. It's not just telling yourself that you believe things will work out and that you will make it. It's determining in your heart that you are going to walk forward and will let God move.

I encourage you to act on your words of faith. Go forward when you reach the other side. Cling to the hope that if God has taken you there, He has planned great things for you there, and He won't leave. His storms often lead to better things. It's our duty to trust Him and obey, to continue living our lives and not wait around. If we do this and have a little faith to bring it to pass, God certainly will.

Let us turn our attention back to the scene described in Matthew 14:34–36. In that specific moment, there was definitely more to the situation than met the eye. But sometimes, we don't look very hard for things we don't believe can happen. Soon enough, God would do His work and perform miracles again. The scripture says that people realized who Jesus was and gathered all who were sick and went to Him. All they had to do was touch the hem of His garment and they were made whole. The scripture doesn't say that every sick person was healed, but every sick person who touched His garment was made whole. Take notice of the fact that all came. Many people were there, and they had to get to Jesus and reach out and touch His garment to be made whole.

They made the effort to put faith into action. The disciples realized that the point of holding on for so long had been for this moment. Isn't it beautiful to know that miracles happen on both sides of the storm, and miracles happen in the middle of the storm if we only learn to cling to and trust His word? How wonderful to know that we can be made whole if we but touch the hem of his garment! His disciples had front-row tickets to one of the first healing services. And if He could do that for strangers and His disciples, surely He can do the same for us!

Surely His touch can heal our aching, weary bodies. Surely His Word can bring joy from our depression. Surely He can speak life into our dead situations, mend broken relationships, and give us clean hearts and renewed minds. Surely He can draw toward Him all people who are weary and heaven-laden, and surely, on the other side, He can give us the rest we have needed for years.

God does things from one shore to the next, and things in-between, and He doesn't ever change. It's important to remember the One who fed the multitudes with such small amounts and provided more than the sum of what they had is the same One who walked on the water. And the One who calmed the storm and rescued His disciples is the same One that will walk with us on the other side.

How can we ever worry when we know the One who has been with us all along and has done miracles and blessed us is the One who will walk with us and show us great and marvelous things? The same God who accomplished what we never expected and the God who never leaves us hungry will be with us. It's very important for us to have a foundation of faith and hope built within us. It's vital to our walk with God; without it, neither we nor He can ever accomplish what He wants to fulfill in our lives. The *perfect* will never be completed in an imperfect, underwhelming way. It will be beautiful. It will be overwhelming and sometimes nauseating. But it will be worth it and when we make it to the other side, it will make our storms seem small and irrelevant.

We may even get to a place in our storms where we shove aside all of our failures, growing pains, frustrations, and questions. Maybe that will be the moment we get to the end of ourselves and worship God all the way to dry land. And on the other side, we may grow to appreciate those storms as we realize God used them to purge everything that was wrong within us. We will realize that He used the storm to transform us and prepare us for the beautiful things that await us.

The other side is where God allows us to see His best work. It is where we will realize that the journey with God was worth it, that we cannot accomplish anything without Him, and that we could never make it without Him. It will become the start and the landmark of our deepest relationship with God. It will also be where God fulfills the things we know He has said to us. It will be where He fulfills His promises to us. The fear, the doubt, the worry—they all seem so small when compared to the palm of His hands, which pull us out of our storms and embrace us. Our human natures and selves seem insignificant compared to His great and marvelous things. The other side is a brand new start, and it is a landmark that shows who has carried us so far. The other side is the place where God is working everything for your good.

All of this will be hard to reach. We will want to try and take control. We'll grow tired, and our hearts and minds will grow weary. Our faith and hope will wane, but I encourage you to hold on and worship God. The other side is where God will always move, and He will get you there. The other side is where miracles happen, and it is where God does His best work, and His promises are fulfilled at last.

Section 2

A Journey Too Long

Who through faith subdued kingdoms, wrought righteousness, obtained promises, stopped the mouths of lions.

—Hebrews 11:33 (KJV)

Chapter 12

God's Promise Renewed

"And it came to pass in process of time that the king of Egypt died: and the children of Israel sighed by reason of the bondage. And God heard their groaning, and God remembered his covenant with Abraham, with Isaac and with Jacob. And God looked upon the children of Israel, and God had respect unto them."

—*Exodus 2:23–25 (KJV)*

It may not seem to make much sense that I am connecting two different stories from two different parts of the Bible, hundreds of years apart, i.e., the disciples during the storm and the Israelites in bondage in Egypt. However, I believe it is important to point out the similarities. I wrote this section to show you that it isn't just Jesus in the New Testament or God in the Old Testament, it is also the Holy Spirit in modern times. It is important and pertinent to know that God doesn't change. He is the same God He has always been, and timeframes do not negate His power, and circumstances certainly do not negate His promises. Though His methods may often differ, He does things in quite similar ways, and they are always done in His perfect timing.

He accomplishes things that seem undoable and cuts down obstacles that seem impenetrable. In both of these incredible stories, God promised to take His people to the other side. He directed the disciples to go to the other shore and showed the

Israelites to the land of promise guaranteed in His covenant with Abraham. In both of these moments, God's people faced circumstances that made it seem as though their prayers had fallen on deaf ears. The circumstances and all the time it took made it seem unlikely that His promises would be fulfilled.

Years and years after God's covenant with Abraham, much was happening. His people had been enslaved for around four hundred years—whipped and abused, living in mockery and shame, ill-treated, subjugated, humiliated, and frustrated. They were underfed, overworked, tired, miserable, sad, and angry, even as they grew used to slavery. I believe it can be very difficult to keep God in one's sights, His Word, and His promises, in the busyness and angst of our normal lives, let alone when all we know for generation after generation is bondage, suffering, early mornings, late nights, and exhaustion. We cannot let this be said of our own lives. I cannot press this matter enough, and I must say it again. We cannot grow so accustomed to our years of pain and hurt that we begin to believe that it's all there is and all there ever will be. God has so much more in store for us.

The truth is, we so often face such troubles, that God hopes we will turn our eyes and hearts toward Him, that we may grow the same unwavering love for Him that He has for us, and that we will trust that He and He alone can take us out of our situations and sustain us. His only desire for us in these moments is for us to realize we need Him and only Him. He is the answer. He is the fulfillment. He is the healer. He is the sustainer. He is our chain breaker. He is our deliverer. He is our restorer, and soon, He will be our guide. He has loved us, and He always will. When we are prisoners to our past or our circumstances and we cannot see Him or hear His voice, we must know that He is waiting for us to turn our eyes upon Him before He moves. He is waiting for us to act spiritually before He acts physically on His promise. He will meet us when we seek Him. He will come to us at the appointed time that He has ordained, and he will turn the problems we have lived with for so long into a pathway to the promises He has made to us. Praise be to Him for such power and faithfulness even when it doesn't seem like He will move. Praise Him in our bondage, praise Him through the storms, and praise Him in the wilderness, because He will appear. He will move, and we will be triumphant!

As the scripture says Exodus 2:24, the Israelites cried out to God because of their bondage and their deplorable situation. Finally, after all this time and all these years, God had heard their groaning. In addition, He remembered His covenant with their forefathers—Abraham, Isaac, and Jacob. Now, do not forget that God is omniscient. God is perfect and He's infallible. He doesn't make mistakes and He never forgets. He knew right where His people were, and He knew they needed to turn to Him. In fact, the Hebrew word in this scripture means not only to recall but also to act upon the remembrance. It is an action verb. At last, after all of the time, toils, and snares, God listened to His people. Why did it seem that God had turned a deaf ear to His people? Why did it seem that they had been ignored and forgotten for so long?

With sincere honesty, I do not believe that was the case at all. I do not believe He needed to be reminded. Psalm 34:17 says, "The righteous cry and the Lord hears, and delivers them out of all their troubles." The Lord remembered what He had promised, and I believe He did not desire to see His chosen people suffer. He didn't want to turn a blind eye to their problems. But I believe, just like in Matthew, He began to orchestrate their preparation for the other side of bondage and even for the other side of the wilderness. Just like in Matthew, God did what was needed to get His people on their way to the other side. As their bondage became too much to handle, they turned to the end of themselves. It took their cries to the Father to obtain their release and change their situation, but they finally had His attention.

God didn't forget His promise at all, and He hadn't forsaken

His people. I do not believe He needed to be reminded; I think God was waiting for the right time. He was waiting for them to be desperate for freedom and even more desperate for Him and for His power, His presence, His love, His grace, His mercy, and His might! He was waiting for them to cry to Him so that they would realize He was all they needed. They were no longer comfortable with accepting bondage. They were sick and tired of it. They were right where God wanted them to be and right where He knew they needed to be. They were finally ready to call on God to show up in their defense, and show up He certainly did. He made His presence known in unimaginable ways, whatever it took for the Israelites' enemy to set them free and to help the Israelites flee from captivity.

Often, though, God selects the person men reject to do what He needs accomplished. This moment and this situation was no different, as He again did the impossible in impossible ways. He chose to use a shy, inadequate, stuttering man named Moses, a man who was not eloquent and seemed too timid to lead anyone, let alone a nation. Yet God chose this man to be the trailblazer into His promises. This man would lead a huge mass of unruly refugees through the desert, keep order, and take them to the border of their future home in Canaan. Before all of that, God used him, along with Aaron, to give an ultimatum to Pharaoh: let God's people go or face serious consequences. Imagine the scene. We all know the story: Moses and Aaron went to Pharaoh, who did not obey. I imagine he chuckled and spit on the ground as he rejected Moses and Aaron and said, "Who is the Lord that I should obey his voice to let Israel go? I know not the Lord, neither will I let Israel go." By speaking those words, Pharaoh challenged God.

Now, we as Christians can see this from two perspectives. We can say we are like the Israelites—waiting in bondage for God to fulfill His promises and perfect plan. For the sake of this book, we will do that, and it's true. Most of us are waiting for God to move and to act on our behalf. I could not agree more with that. If we think about it though, we will realize that sometimes we play the part of Pharaoh—either in the lives of others or in our own. We face a dilemma, and in a moment's time, we forget all the things He is. We neglect all the things we talked about in section 1, and we forget who He is; we often challenge God.

But Yahweh, as He always perfectly does, stood true to His word, and He certainly made Himself known. He turned Egypt's water into blood and killed their fish. Nothing changed. Frogs invaded the land; nothing changed. The list goes on and on. God sent lice, flies, a plague that wiped out the livestock, boils, hail, locusts, and darkness that could be felt. Still, nothing changed. Finally, when these things didn't work, God sent the plague of death for every firstborn child whose household had not put blood over the door.

Pharaoh's son died, as did many Egyptian children. The Egyptians feared they were next in line for death and gave all they could to get the Israelites out of their land. The Israelites not only were allowed to leave Egypt, they were ultimately commanded by Pharaoh to do so. The Bible says that there were 600,000 men, in addition to women and children, who left that night. They did not leave broken, struggling, hurting, scared, or defeated, friend. They didn't leave empty handed or with half-full baskets. No! They left greatly enriched by the Egyptians. This ended 430 years of the children of Israel dwelling in Egypt in bondage and slavery. This was the beginning of many long days in the desert. This all was the beginning of their journey into the land that God had promised them for decades.

Now, this chapter is not about Moses. It is about the Israelites, and it's about us. Moses was simply the tool God used to get His chosen people on their way. He was the hand, Aaron was the mouth, and God was the mastermind. That is how much He loved them, and that is how much God loves us. He sends people our way to guide us to where we need to go, and He plans everything before we ever face the circumstances. He speaks His promises before we ever face the problems, and since He knows the results, isn't it easier to trust Him in the middle of the trial? Isn't it easier to trust His faithfulness than to trust our doubts and listen to our fears? No doubt, the answer should be yes, and it may even start off that way. But just like the Israelites, even after we call on His name and finally turn to Him, our human nature ultimately kicks in and we begin to doubt along the way.

There will be times when God gives us a promise, a vision, a dream, a longing! Then all of a sudden and out of nowhere, God goes silent, and we cannot hear His voice. We cry and pray and weep, and we hear nothing from Him. It seems as if all our words and prayers have fallen on deaf ears, until the moment of fulfillment final begins to rear its head. There will be times when someone comes along and completely disrupts what God had planned. People will come and lie to you and about you. They will cast their stones. Some will try to discourage you.

No doubt Job experienced this when his friends told him turn from God and accused him of sins. Circumstances and people will distract you and cause you to forget God's promises. At times, we will be prisoners to self-deprecation. We will moan and complain to God. We will cry "woe is me" and ignore the fact that we can call on God for help. Sometimes we will be prisoners to doubt and worry and fear. There will be times when our prison chambers become those of disappointment. We will be trapped in moments of disbelief about our promises being fulfilled. The list goes on and on. Some people and things will make you feel too inadequate for God's blessings to be fulfilled in your life.

Guess what? The truth is that you are. You don't deserve anything God has promised you. The Israelites didn't deserve anything but prison, but this promise remained prevalent in their lives. Even when they forgot about it, God did something amazing. He renewed His promise and fulfilled something that probably seemed too good to be true. Have you ever been at such a point in your life, when you felt unworthy and undeserving and believed that nothing could make you worthy of His blessings and promises? Have you ever been in awe of Him as he provided and accomplished His work and whispered to yourself, *This is too good to be true* or *after all I've done, I don't deserve this*? Can I share with you a simple truth? Although it is true that you are not good enough and are too inadequate to obtain God's promises, it is also a fact that when it seems too good to be true, that's because it is. It's called grace, and God is grace. You can do everything and still deserve nothing, but He loves you enough to always fulfill His promises.

There will come a moment when God provides a ram or sends a reminder or another Moses to get us where He wants us to go. God always uses people to help us along the way, sometimes to guide and direct us. At other times, He shows us His capabilities and might through the things He accomplishes in our lives. He is reminding us, through our doubt and worry, that He has done it before and that He is able!

My point is, do not lose heart so easily. Yes, the enemy will attack—physically and mentally. He will cast shadows of doubt over our heads. He will cause us to lose focus, and positive change will seem unlikely. It will seem that we will never overcome challenges and there is no way out, but there is. Always, always remember that circumstances change, but God's promises do not. There is a consequence to disobedience. There is a result to our sins. There is a price we must pay when we run from God, and there is a price when we try to hide. Running away can and will change the circumstances around us. But it will never change the promises of God. If we only learn to turn 180 degrees back to God and learn to obey Him, He will remind us about His promises to us. If we learn to be like the Israelites when they cried to Him, He will move, and there will be times when we must cry out to God as well. Confusion will set in. Worry, doubt, and fear can easily settle in our hearts and the inability to stop overthinking and simply obey can truly stagnate our movement forward. But we must continue to take our steps as He leads us to the other side, and we must not ever forget that the journey is never easy but is always worth it.

Chapter 13

Why Do We Remain Wilderness Wanderers?

"And the Lord's anger was kindled against Israel, and he made them wander in the wilderness forty years, until all the generation that had done evil in the sight of the Lord was consumed."

—Numbers 32:13 (KJV)

"For the children of Israel walked forty years in the wilderness, till all the people that were men of war, which came out of Egypt, were consumed, because they obeyed not the voice of the Lord: unto whom the Lord swore that he would not shew them the land, which the Lord swore unto their fathers that he would us, a land that floweth with milk and honey."

—Joshua 5:6 (KJV)

I know this is a lot of scripture to read, but as I began studying this story, skipping from book to book and praying about what scripture to use, I ultimately found that it was pertinent to cover both biblical passages. I recall the moment, months after our storm had begun, and we were still enduring. I kept asking God if He would heal my sister or mend our broken hearts or meet me on a personal level as I had some needs of my own. Some nights I would be so angry; I was always asking God why He kept speaking to me about holding onto the things I was hoping for even though it was eating me up inside. I was so weary of it. My family was weary. My friends were weary of hearing about it.

I was mentally and spiritually exhausted. I had found myself there before, and Christians always will find themselves there at one time or another. We've been heartbroken, lost, and confused; walking around in our misery and our complaining. We demand that God end the things we were going through or fulfill the things He said He would, that He take away the hope of things turning around or bring them to pass. Sometimes, all we ever want is an end. The waiting and the walking was agonizing for me, and it may be that way for you too. For me, it was uncomfortable, and it didn't seem right. I was weary of the unknown, yet that is exactly where I had been for so long. *Is He going to heal? Is He not? Is He going to restore? Is He not? Is there a purpose in all of this? How much longer until we are there?* Oh, I had questions. Did I ever! Then one day at work, as I was going about my day, a question dawned on me:

Why do we remain wilderness wanderers?

I'm obviously not talking about a literal wilderness. I'm talking about the journey that sends us on our way to the promises God has told us and laid on our hearts. Why do we dwell in hurting and heartache, and how long do we wish to walk in circles?! How long must we go through the same cycle, time and time again? Why do we remain wilderness wanderers? Allow me to give you with a few potential reasons by taking you back to the beginning in Exodus 14.

Fear and Lack of Faith

This is not the first time the Israelites have been scared, and it certainly will not be the last. God has already begun answering their cries, as He has commanded them to flee and Moses to lead His people to freedom. God has been faithful all this time, but they cannot see that. He has blessed His people, answered them, gave them direction, and He has begun to step in and take over. But don't you know it? The enemy attacks them again. There is a saying, "When the enemy attacks you, a blessing is at hand." The enemy attacks valiantly, at every opportunity, and seemingly at the most perfect times during the Israelites' journey. Again, they have lived in bondage for longer than some of them knew, but this is their first time to be attacked in freedom. Just when things should have looked up, they have the enemy on their backs, charging full force after them. The Israelites face overwhelming odds that they will even survive to make it to the other side.

Does that sound at all familiar to you? Does the enemy attack you when you are right on the cusp of victory, when it seems that you've almost made it? Does the enemy run headlong at you when there seems to be no way of escape? Does he send every bad thing your way? Are you fearful for your life or about the outcome of certain events?

Do not lose heart, friend. The Lord will never send you through the desert to destroy you. The dry, barren, quiet, dying land is not your destination. It's not the end of your life, and it is not some bad omen signifying where you are going. It also does not indicate of God's unfulfilled promise. It is simply a pathway to your promise and a means to the other side. Do not prolong your journey by being fearful, and do not ever allow fear to give birth to your lack of faith. In verse 11 of Exodus 14, the people ask Moses, "because there were no graves in Egypt, have you taken us away to die in the wilderness?" In verse 12, they basically say to him, "Did we not tell you in Egypt to leave us alone so that we may serve the Egyptians? For it was better for us to serve the Egyptians than to die in the wilderness?" They have such little faith that they are willing to live in bondage and with the enemy. They are willing to serve the enemy and let the enemy control them. They are willing to let the enemy and their circumstances dictate their lives. They re willing to stay slaves than to go all out in their obedience to God—all because they have no faith. God has done for them time and time again, but they are ungrateful and are never pleased with God's ways.

Later on in their journey, they are miraculously fed manna from heaven every day, although they complain that Aaron and Moses have taken them into the desert to starve to death. Once again, as I mentioned in the first section, God feeds a multitude of people with seemingly nothing. Mere mortals eat the bread of the Almighty God and drink from the water of the everlasting, as if the water itself is from His limitless depths. He sends them as much as they can ever want. He makes a way of survival for them when there isn't one, and He makes it easier than they deserve. He keeps their clothes from wearing out and their feet from swelling. He does this throughout the extremely long trip. He gently escorts the Israelites through their journey in the desert wilderness in the form of a cloud by day and a pillar of fire by night. He provides for the Israelites' every need. He shows them how awesome and amazing He is. All the while, He is teaching them to trust Him, rely on Him, and be obedient to His commands, and it all began when He set them free. That alone should convince them that God will follow through, regardless of how dim things look. But the people do not praise Him. They don't lift their hands in thankfulness and adoration for what God has done on their way to the land of milk and honey. This was the test, just as in Matthew, when the disciples came face to face with water. Often, we in our fragile faith only see the impassible water in our lives. I have even had moments when it almost seems abnormal to have faith.

Imagine the scene. These people have just escaped from a

place where they have been enslaved for so long, it became their home. To some, it is all they have ever known, and though they were slaves, they still had their homes and their families. We can grow so used to living among our enemies—of living with hurt, failure, mistakes, and so forth—that even though it's tough, we find comfort in the fact that we at least have something. The thought is, *This is awful, but I would rather be bound by this than be dead.* That is the most dangerous place to be as a Christian, when we forget that God has more for us than just hurt and pain and "just living." He wants us to prosper and to trust Him to fulfill what He says He will.

In any case, the Israelites flee from all they had known for so long. Many are mumbling and grumbling under their breath, shaking their fists passionately. The men yank their stubborn cattle behind them. The children complain about every little thing. And the women—oh, the women—are sick of their husbands telling them what to do: keep walking, slow down, stand up, sit down, and keep the kids quiet. Tempers flare, and doubt, panic, and exhaustion kick in, but they still move to get as far away, as soon as possible, from their past of bondage. Perhaps many of them have smiles on their faces as they think that they have finally made it out. Then just as they begin to pick up speed due to the pure elation and adrenaline pumping through their veins, they notice their feet are wet. They hear the splashing water before they realize they were doomed. There is no way they can escape the years of bondage they'd endured. *How dare God ever give us a promise that doesn't come easy?* Does that sound familiar to you? Have you thought the same thing? *But God, you've promised me this. Why is it such a struggle?* I've said it once myself. But the Israelites accuse Moses of sending them out there to die. There is water before them and multitudes of people in their group, many of them children. They have an eighty-year-old leader, who needs a staff to get around and stutters through his words. They do not have weapons, and an army is close behind them. Surely, this is the end of everything they knew. Surely this means they either go back to slavery or die. It certainly looks as though they face insurmountable odds.

Once more though, God steps in when they don't deserve it, and He is right on time. He is always right on time. Moses comes to God's defense. "The Lord will fight for you," he says, and boy was he right. In Exodus 14:15, God, in turn, gives Moses direct instructions to speak to the Israelites and tell them to go forward. He tells Moses to lift up his rod, stretch out his hand over the Red Sea, and divide it so that the children of Israel may go on dry land through the middle of the sea. God blesses those who are obedient, and God always provides a way out. God, true to His word, separates the water and makes a pathway when there wasn't one.

My question to you is, what does God need to divide in your life to get you to the other side? The sea of regret? The sea of abandonment and hurt? The sea of brokenness? The sea of addiction? The waters may seem too much to walk through, and that may be true for some. But you can watch as God separates them in your life, just as Moses did with his staff. As Moses lifted up his staff to the Lord, so too must we lift up our hands and worship Him. Worship is to victory as breathing is to life. Do not grow angry and weary with God on your way through your wilderness. Build a relationship with God. Don't be like the Israelites and feed your spirit of disbelief. Look around you at the things God does to prepare you for the journey. Watch Him as He removes the obstacles from your path. Let Him do the unexplainable.

The Israelites walk through the water, on dry land, all the way to the other side, while the enemy behind them is swept away, never to be seen again. This Sea of Forgetfulness is where our past hurts go in order to die. It is a monument to what we were supposed to overcome and to what God can do, a remembrance of all we were but were never meant to be. It takes all of this for the Israelites to fear the Lord and to believe the Lord.

Surely, this was a turning point in their attitude toward God. So, why was this only the beginning? How did they escape from the enemy, make it through the Red Sea, and all the way to the other side? In addition to God using Moses to split the waters, what else got them on their way? It wasn't the deep waters splitting open; that was merely a pathway. It wasn't Moses lifting his staff up to God. It wasn't some deep formula or some crazy code. It was God's instruction to go forward and their obedience in their steps. They needed to go forward—yes, even though they moaned, complained, and had their doubts—to experience God moving like He did. Otherwise, they never would have gotten to the other side and ultimately to Canaan. Sometimes, we have to keep moving—even when it hurts, it doesn't make much sense, we cannot comprehend His direction, we are aching, and we do not know or understand why we are going through our trials. We have to keep going forward, or we will never experience God's beautiful, perfect and ultimate plan. We will never experience the miracles of God. If you don't want to dwell in the wilderness, you cannot look at the task in front of you and think about impossibilities. You cannot lose your trust in Him and grow fearful, but you must keep going forward!

So, why did they walk through the wilderness for forty years? Just like disciples in the boat, disbelief had taken up residence. Could it be that because of their disbelief in God's ways and His powers that their hearts inherited disobedience?

Laziness, Impatience, and Complacency

Could it be that more than fear and a lack of faith kept them in the wilderness? Did laziness and complacency have just as much to do with it? Numbers 32 tells us that after they make it through the

Red Sea, and truly begin their journey, they head to the lands of Jazer and Gilead. They watch as God creates a country for them and see that it is great land for their cattle. They even ask Moses if they have found grace and so may inherit the land and not cross over the river Jordan. This is complacency, caused by laziness and rooted in impatience. How ignorant the Israelites are. They take advantage of the things God does for them.

I remember studying this scripture and thinking about their apparent lack of intelligence. How could they try and take advantage of God and do things their way after He had shown so much grace toward them, after He restored His promise to them. They didn't deserve the Promised Land, and they certainly didn't deserve this land of cattle they were asking for. But just as I began to look at them in this light, God softly pricked my heart. As I wondered how the Israelites gained such confidence to ask God for something He had not promised them—especially after all their moaning and complaining—I realized I was describing myself. This is often how we behave in moments of longing. We want God to fulfill His promises, but we do not want to do the work that it entails. We do not want to endure or overexert our energy in order to do our part, nor do we want to just move forward and wait.

Once I prayed to God for something. I put down a fleece before Him and sat in prayer. I worshipped Him and did my best to believe He would fulfill my request. I sat back and watched as it began to come together and then watched as it seemed to fall apart. Just like these Israelites, I had been on my way to the Promised Land. I was on my way to my promise. You probably are too, and the truth is that perhaps it takes longer than we want it to. Perhaps we face harder obstacles than we anticipated, and maybe we grow tired and disheartened. Perhaps you've even questioned if the end will justify the means during this journey. As I was on my way, I thought, *Well, this promise doesn't seem likely anymore. I'm not even sure if it's worth it after all of this.* I told myself,

God, if you'll just do this for me and if you'll just give me this, then I'll be okay. This is exactly what the Israelites did, and God gave them what they wanted. In my case, thank God loves me enough not to always give me what I want.

Consider the response Moses gives to the Israelites in Numbers 32:6. He asks them if they will sit there while their brothers go to war. Moses is on to them; he knows they are lazy and complacent. And do you know what God does? He grows so angry that He not only makes the Israelites walk through the wilderness for forty years, He denies the adults among them access to the Promised Land. Except for Joshua and Caleb, those who are twenty years and older will not inherit the land of milk and honey. Those who want the land of cattle get what they want, but they never get the best that God has planned for them—all because they have grown complacent, impatient, and lazy. They don't desire to keep fighting. They don't desire to keep following God. They are willing to sit back and miss out on God's plan. They are willing to settle for the land of cattle instead of striving for the land of milk and honey. They refuse to follow God wholly.

This is the last thing that will cause you to remain a wilderness wanderer: refusing to follow God wholly, that is, to do exactly what the Israelites did. They no longer trusted, no longer believed, no longer willing to fight. They settled, moaning and complaining. How can we expect God to do His part when we cannot do ours? We must only trust and obey. The task is simple, and yet we struggle to do it! I guess the real question is, how do we escape the wilderness? It certainly is a pressing matter. It's a hard one for us, with our finite minds, to fully answer, but could the answer be less formulaic than we think? Could the answer simply be to follow God wholly? That is to say, with our whole hearts and with confidence in Him. Without complacency but with great expectancy. Not just when things are going right but in our daily walk. Not traveling under the light of our own wisdom but under His guidance. Walking upright and not sitting down.

Seth Ramey

Joshua and Caleb walked upright, and they not only made it to the Promised Land, they played a big part in helping to fulfill God's promises to the Israelites. They conquered overwhelming odds and lived long enough to enjoy their successes. They found favor by walking wholly in the sight of God and were blessed for it. My prayer for you is that you commit to walking wholly before The Lord and that you will not settle for less than His best. Thank Him for not giving you want you want, and know that He will not withhold any good thing from His people who walk upright.

Chapter 14

When Things Don't Add Up

The title of this chapter may seem similar to the title of chapter 4, "When Things Don't Make Sense," and that's because it is. I think it's encouraging to know that it wasn't just the disciples who went against what God had promised them. The Israelites, including Joshua and Caleb, did the same. As they walked through the desert, they were confused and annoyed and wondered about the schedule and direction of God. As the entire generation that didn't make it was disobedient and despondent, I can only imagine Joshua and Caleb wondering why they had been walking for so many years.

Nothing measured up to God's promise to them. In fact, wandering in the wilderness seemed to go against His word and contravene everything. None of it made an ounce of sense, and nothing added up to God's promises. How discouraged they must have felt, how defeated, how neglected and incompetent. They were unable to piece anything together, as none of the pieces seemed to fit together for God's plan.

Why was it harder for them to get where God wanted them to be? The sad thing is that most of their obstacles were self-inflicted, and they probably didn't even yet realize it. I'm sure many of them realized things weren't adding up as they began to doubt that God's promise would be fulfilled. There was no way it could be. Certainly, they would not reach the Promised Land, the land flowing with milk and honey—not when giants were standing in their way. I wonder if perhaps some of the faithful few, for just a split second, thought to themselves, *we are so small and exhausted from walking so long. How can we ever muster enough strength to conquer these giants in our way?* But, the power to make it, even when nothing else added up, was right there with them. They just forgot that when it didn't make sense to them and they didn't have quick fixes and shortcuts, God knew what was going on. The same hands that created the heavens and the earth could put everything together. They forgot that God was their guide and would never lead them astray.

The good news is that it's not just about the Israelites or the disciples. It was, is, and always will be about us! We can sit back and reminisce about the times God pointed us in a direction and said go, and we can remember the times we stood, disheveled, on the shore or wandered through the proverbial wilderness thinking about how, when, and where His promises will be fulfilled. We've tried to fix our problems, resolve them, and mend them our way. At times, we've attempted to piece things together and have completely failed, blaming God because we've made matters worse. We've grown irritated because we do not always know the step-by-step plan that God has for our journey, although we should just learn to trust Him at His word. We grow discouraged when every step of progress is followed or accompanied by a stumbling block, and it seems to make no sense to trust God or to continue onward. The struggle doesn't seem right, and we want to give up as our minds keep racing.

This can cause us to grow angry and to feel hurt. I've found myself asking, *What am I supposed to do when things don't add up?* Maybe you've asked the exact same question. My family has been there, and in such moments, I've allowed my mind to wander more than it ever should. It seemed like my life would progress perfectly. I made huge advances. I listened to God. I heard Him whisper His promises and felt Him lay things on my heart. My family took major, monumental steps forward and then suddenly, they were dashed, and we felt like we'd taken two steps back.

I've heard testimony after testimony after testimony from people who went through the hardest trials of their lives while they were waiting for God to fulfill His promises—things seemed completely opposite to what He'd said to them. I listened to these testimonies all the way through until they spoke about how God did what He said He would do. I listened as God brought hope, peace, and confidence to them during their trials. Yet there I was, doubting everything He'd said to me.

I not only doubted His promises to me, I doubted God Himself. I questioned His character, believing that He'd led me on, manipulated me, and perhaps even lied to me. We've all been there, and even many of the famous Bible characters faced these lowly points in their lives. David, the man after God's own heart, waited years before he was appointed king. He worked as a shepherd, and he was hunted by the king, while living as a fugitive with his very future in doubt. Being a shepherd and facing all of these things was completely opposite to what a king should go through. It didn't add up, but God appointed him king, God promised David his throne, and God stayed true to His word. Isn't it good to know that we are not alone? The greatest of Christ's followers have suffered moments of confusion and turmoil, and we can use such moments to remind us that He'll see us through, and that we don't stand alone.

I honestly cannot explain why these things happen. I can't tell you why things don't add up and seemingly go against His promises. I can't tell you why you aren't getting the healing or the church growth or seeing your future take place the way you believed He promised would happen. I can't tell you how to stop the confusion or turmoil, or when it stops. I don't have an equation or recipe for how to get there. What I do know is that God is ever faithful, even when it doesn't seem that way. What if I told you this is exactly where God wanted you to be? No, I'm not talking about questioning Him. I'm not talking about wandering minds and angry, broken hearts. I am not talking about the confusion and the finger-pointing at God.

I'm talking about God wanting us to be in the exact place in our lives where nothing adds up—where nothing comes together, nothing seems to fit, and we throw our hands up in surrender. It is there, in that moment—when we have no idea at all and we have done all we can to manipulate our way to achieving His promises—that we step aside and hand the reigns back over to the One who can speak life into a dead situation. He wants us there with all of our faith invested in Him, to completely entrust Him with the power to guide us, to realize that it is only through Him and by Him that we receive His promise. We cannot do one thing on our own. We cannot create an answer out of dust from the ground. No! We can do nothing, and we must give Him control of our journey. We must give him control of our minds and reassure ourselves that when there are no answers, He has them all.

The truth is, everything He promises His people is a gift to us, but it still belongs to God. It was molded in His hands, formed from His word, kept by His faithfulness and we are merely the recipients. It is by His grace alone that we ever obtain blessings or gifts from Him. It is by His love for us that we ever retain them. That is quite a humbling thought, isn't it?

If we can only keep hold of that and step aside, then we can entrust the Lord of all to guide us to His promise. It is the act of absolute true faith. Maybe we should step aside with no questions asked and maybe we ought to take Him at His word and trust His ways. I don't have all the answers and directions for you. I don't even have all of them for myself. However, over the past few years, I've met plenty of people who have used their present situations to change their perspectives about the character of God. Once I tried to encourage a friend who was going through a big problem in his life, and he told me he wasn't sure what God was up to anymore. That ate at me. He told me he was having a hard time trusting God and believing Him and in Him. It reminded me of myself at one point in my life and how the Israelites in the wilderness messed up. I was having a conversation with someone very close to me about this, and this is what he said: "True Christian faith never relies on the situations or problems we face; it relies upon the very character of God, and within His character lies the absolute inability to fail."

Maybe you and your family have really faced it this past year or for the past three years. Maybe the world seems to be spiraling out of control around you. Perhaps there has been a monumental collapse of hope in your life, and it seems that when it rains it, really pours, and nothing makes any sense. But let me encourage you with this: hardships and struggles, though they seem counter to God's promises, do not negate God's promises, and they certainly do not negate the character of God. God is truth, and God is faithful, so when He said He would do something—such lead His people to the Promised Land or make David king—He meant it. His character doesn't change; men and their faith do. That is where the problem really lies.

Nothing added up in the wilderness, and that is exactly where God wanted them. It is where He wants us. But God's character remains, and thank God, His ways are not our ways. Thank God His thoughts are not our thoughts, because if He doubted and feared like the Israelites did, if He, the God of all, worried like we did, we all surely would be doomed. God has a lot of weight on His shoulders. The faith of the Israelites was shaken to its core, yet His character never once wavered. It never wavers. When nothing seems at all to add up, trust in the flawless character of God, trust in His sovereign power, and believe in His infallible word.

Yes, the Israelites made some very serious mistakes in the wilderness. They acted out of emotion. They said and did ignorant things simply because they were confused and untrusting of God even when He provided food, protected them, and delivered them out of slavery. Even Moses himself had failed at one point, but the Israelites were obedient in some aspects. They did get up and flee and do exactly what they were commanded; they did follow the pillar of cloud and the one of fire. Yet they went through all these hardships. They faced all these obstacles and dangers and confusion. Although God had protected them every step of the way, they grew confused and irritable that they had not yet reached the Promised Land.

The Israelites were in the will of God but in a difficult time. It is possible and even very likely to be in the will of God and also in a season of great problems. It is possible to be in His will and not have every step be crystal clear. God gives promises, and He always keeps them. Yet God never said there wouldn't be battles. He never said it would be easy, and He certainly never said it would go the way you want it to. But He did say He'd get you there. He said He wouldn't leave you, and He said that you can make it. So, keep going, even when it doesn't make sense. Trust in His sovereign hand, even when you don't always know what is in it, and trust in His all-seeing eye when you cannot see clearly. Trust His character in which exists the inability to fail.

Chapter 15

God's Breadcrumbs

"And gavest them bread from heaven for their hunger, and broughtest forth water for them out of the rock for their thirst, and promisedst them that they should go in to possess the land which thou hadst sworn to give them."

—Nehemiah 9:15 (KJV)

"And the Lord went before them by day in a pillar of a cloud, to lead them the way; and by night in a pillar of fire, to give them light; to go by day and night."

—Exodus 13:21 (KJV)

First of all, yes. The title of this chapter is a playful reference to the miracle of manna. I find it fitting that during the entire journey God fed His people with bread from heaven; morning after morning, He sprinkled the ground with bread for them to eat. No doubt, there was a trail of breadcrumbs. But to take a more serious note, have you ever had a moment in your life, perhaps after you've walked through your wilderness for a while? Maybe it happens in the middle of your struggles, after you've gone through the emotions and questioned "what's the use" and "is it really worth it." Or you experience long days where nothing adds up or makes sense. Then, maybe long after the initial loss of faith, step by step, breath by breath, and moment by moment, things seem to slowly but surely fall into place. I'm not talking about the moment when God brings forth His promise in your life or you see the "light at the end of the tunnel," if you will. I'm talking about the little breadcrumbs that He seems to drop in front of you, simple reminders that He hasn't forgotten about you or the promise He gave you. He has not left you but is working, moving, orchestrating things, and preparing you for what is yet to come. Perhaps He is strengthening you for the head-on collision you will have with God's promises.

These little breadcrumbs from God give us steps of clarity, renewal of faith, and a renewed hope that He and His faithful character will see us and His promises through to the end. If we are faithful and obedient to Him, if we learn to truly walk wholly with God, then He will do just that—see us through to the end. There is a saying, "it's hard to see the forest because of the trees"; if we are not careful, if we do not fix our eyes and ears on what God says and what He is trying to show us, this saying can become the theme of our lives, what we are known and remembered by. But it also may be the very thing that prevents us from getting to the other side. We can grow too involved in the details of our problems, our situations, and our storms, to look at the situation as a whole. We can focus only on the small, dreary details and fail to understand the larger plans or principles God is trying to show us and lead us to.

At several times on their journey, the Israelites focused on the bad situations, on always being on the run, and dwelling in the wilderness. It didn't just distract them, however; it impaired, discouraged, and exhausted them. It caused them to waver. They were so caught up in the wilderness that they could not see all that God was doing. They shut their ears off to Him, and their memories seemed to fail them. They didn't praise God for taking them out of the desert. Even when they mentioned it, it was with disgust or to accuse God for creating their current situation. That is why many of them never made it to the Promised Land. They asked God if He'd freed them from slavery so they would die in the wilderness. They did not consider the character of God. They deserved to be slaves and to die in bondage, but God still tried to get their attention!

Because the Israelites begged to be delivered from bondage, God fulfilled this giant miracle in an undoubtedly dramatic fashion. When they faced the Red Sea and an army charging full force at them, God did for the Israelites what He did for the disciples: He took them through the waters. Just as Jesus fed the crowd, as described in the book of Matthew, when the Israelites needed food to eat, God provided manna from heaven. When they needed water, He told Moses to strike a rock, and water flowed forth. He kept their shoes and clothes from rotting, and when they needed direction, didn't know where to go, and were turned around and beyond confused, God guided them. He was their cloud by day and their fire by night. God slowly gave the younger generation the strength and faith they needed to conquer other nations and make their way to their land of promise. God raised Joshua and Caleb to lead the generation that would finally enter into the Promised Land. He knew that the two men had what it took and rewarded them for being obedient to Him and for having the faith they needed. God used some pretty significant breadcrumbs to remind them, don't you think? Ultimately, Joshua and Caleb's faith kept God's promise alive and the rest of the Israelites moving onward. The promise essentially lived on through them! Isn't it a beautiful thing to know that because of faith—when things look dreary and hopeless, when you ignore the breadcrumbs and your circumstances seem to be taking their victory lap, and even when you don't truly deserve His promises—He guides us anyway? This is because He helped raise in you the faith to trust and be strong in Him.

I believe God brings things our way that are meant to

encourage us and keep us going forward. He sometimes drops breadcrumbs before us to help us put one foot in front of the other. Have you been there? You are facing the storm of your life and your health or something else has taken a turn for the worse. You cry out for God to heal you, restore your marriage and relationships, or just to turn this situation of yours around. Seemingly out of nowhere, the preacher offers a sermon on healing or deliverance or restoration, although you've never mentioned a word about our problem to anyone. Maybe a mentor sends you incredible words of advice that encourage you to hold on and keep pushing forward. Perhaps someone testifies about overcoming a situation that is similar to yours, while you sit there in a puddle of tears and a lot more faith. I believe God can send things your way to remind you the promise He has told your heart about. I have written down a list of ways He has done this in my life, and it is the biggest reason why I pursued publishing this book. Sometimes, through those little breadcrumbs, God in all of His awesome, perfect and wonderful glory slowly brings everything together.

Here is the disclaimer: it isn't because of the signs and little breadcrumbs that we should fully trust in God. That is not always faith. Faith comes by hearing the Word of God. It is not when I neglect God's Holy Word that He shows me these "breadcrumbs."

But often when I am lost in His Word, on time, faithful to church, and spending a little longer in prayer, people come my way, a word of encouragement is spoken, my perspective begins to change, and I start to see things happen. What I am trying to say is absorb all of God and His Word that you can during your wilderness wandering. Study His Word. Take Him at His word, and don't neglect the things He does to remind you about His promises. Believe in them, and follow after them.

We can go back to the character aspect of God and realize with a great deal of assurance that God wasn't going to do all those things for the Israelites so they would wander in the desert for no purpose and for no reason. He wouldn't say something and then change His mind. God doesn't lie. He wouldn't keep doing miracles and extraordinary things so they could die or remain there. He wouldn't keep showing them His grace, mercy, and love just to watch them waste away—not when something greater awaited them, not when His promise wasn't fulfilled. Through the hardships, He was preparing them to take that land! And because some of them would not take Him at His word, God showed them daily that not only was He going to move but that He was moving! He showed up, stepped in and went before them. That is what faith and devotion to Him can do. That is what the journey and the breadcrumbs can do. Prepare you.

I would like to ask you the very same thing. Through your journey of suffering and hardship and as you follow the breadcrumbs, what is God preparing *you* for? What bigger thing awaits you? Is the preparation for your healing, or restoration for the years of broken marriage you've endured, or deliverance from a life you've given into for far too long? Is it church growth or simply a deeper walk with God? Is it the desire and vision to work for His kingdom? What is the Lord preparing you for? What is He shaping you for? Follow the breadcrumbs that God is sending your way. Let Him nourish you to keep going, let Him be your guide, let Him remind you that He is most definitely going to move. Trust that He will never take back His word and that He will go before you! God used breadcrumbs to start preparing and strengthening the Israelites to take the Promised Land. Just like the Israelites were fed, God is not going to sustain you, give you strength and sustenance simply to let it go to waste. He isn't going to let you wander through the desert in pain and suffering so he can leave you there, not when He is feeding and nurturing you. If the Lord didn't want you to make it, He wouldn't play games. He wouldn't give you the strength to keep going, but He has. Take advantage of that strength! Use it to persevere, and use it to achieve your promise!

I would like you to reflect on these three questions:

1) What is He preparing *you* for?
2) What is your promised land?
3) What little things has God has done to remind you of these two goals?

For some of you, I imagine questions 1 and 2 have the same answer. If you have thought about the answers for awhile, I encourage you to write them down and pray about them. Praise and glorify God in advance, and let Him have His way. Let Him guide the way, and allow the God of All to work in the way He chooses to work. Keep your eyes open and alert and your ears sensitive to His voice, and let Him bless you, because the destination will be far greater than the journey. The breadcrumbs will lead you into something marvelous, and all the battles, waves, and dry lands will look so small in contrast to the promise He said He would accomplish. Heed His breadcrumbs, but know they will never go against His word. Reflect on these breadcrumbs as you read the rest of this book, and ask yourself if any of them remind you of your own life.

Chapter 16

Getting to Where God Wants Us

"And let us not be weary in well doing: for in due season we shall reap, if we faint not."

—Galatians 6:9 (KJV)

I will not cite a lot of scripture that specifically touches on the theme of this chapter but instead will focus on the actions of Joshua and Moses. Where does God want us to be? It is one of the questions the devil attacked me with, and I had to ask God about it in prayer. I talked to one of my friends about it, and we realized that most of us, as people and Christians, face this question when we seem to be living life aimlessly and without purpose. It arrives in the forefront of our minds and is often accompanied with dry spells, silent times, hardships, and obstacles. This question is attached to the feeling of uselessness and longing, making us feel as if we were destined to walk in circles for years at a time and like the desert isn't the road but our destination.

Have you ever wondered how you are supposed to get where God wants you? Have you ever wondered why you feel confused, battered, bruised, and as though you're wasting away? You seem so far away from God and the blessings He gives or the promises He spoke about. You no longer feel sheltered in His arms or the comfort of His guidance but as though you must go it alone. I know I certainly have felt this way.

For a year I thought a lot about how to get to where God

wants me to be. I talked to my friend, and this is what we came up with: you end up where you are supposed to be by doing what you are supposed to do and by doing the right thing when you are given the opportunity. It is a matter of "making the right choices," if you will. Not everything is black and white. The world and society will do their hardest to blur the lines, and they have. We sometimes have to make some very hard decisions in our lives, but that is exactly where grace comes in. I have confidence that if you keep striving to do the right thing, you'll end up exactly where God wants you to be in the exact moment He wants you there.

I also think doing right is a big deal. God is always creating escape routes for His people. He did it for the Israelites when they were in bondage and when they were in the desert. He did it in the examples discussed in chapter 15. God is making a way of escape for you right now. In essence, the opportunity to make a wrong decision is a testament to the fact that a right decision can also be made. There is always a choice, and making the decision is hardly ever easy. Now, our theory is that making right choices will land you right in the middle of God's will. It doesn't matter if your human eyes can't see the end result or your mind can't understand how it will to work together for good. God says it will work if you love Him; you just have to keep being pliable in His hands. He always reveals His plan step by step, not according to a roadmap. We probably wouldn't need to talk with Him every day if He just handed us the full plan in a neat and tidy way. His plans and promises always, always seem to be a beautiful mystery right up to the moment they come to fruition. Life is far better the way He does it—even when it doesn't seem that way, even when it doesn't look promising, even when it doesn't look hopeful—and it's definitely more adventurous. It is certainly more exciting, and it is always worth it!

The truth is there are times on this road when you won't know where to go, when you stand alone, and the obstacles in front of you seem impassible. Those are very heavy moments in life. You may be beyond doubting and questioning whether God will fulfill your promises. But perhaps you'll think, *I've never passed this way before* or *I didn't know it would take me through this or happen this way,* and you will feel like you need a hand to hold. However, in these moments, it is important to remind yourself that you know that God will get you there if you continue doing what is right. Joshua and Caleb were the only two who believed in God's promises and chose to cling to them.

They were some of the only people who didn't disobey and forsake God. They were the two who didn't disagree with God, the two who put the Lord first, even before God's promises to them. They were the two who had confidence that they could conquer the giants. They were the only ones who had the faith to keep walking when others wanted to stop. They didn't question God. They believed in God's promises! They faced a series of choices, and they made the right choice time and again. They seemed to live for the right decisions. I'm not saying they were perfect, but they strived toward perfection. I wonder how ridiculed they were at times. How often were they mocked? Did people spit on them and call them ignorant children? Did some people cross them off as do-gooders and talk to them as though they would never accomplish anything? The list goes on and on. There will be times in your life when you know beyond the shadow of a doubt that what God promised you will be accomplished and you will continue living in preparation for it. But people around you will laugh and mock you for it. Some will tell you you're wrong. Some will tell you to move on and give it up. Some will encourage you to be realistic while pointing out that others haven't seen the promise or seen "things change." There will be times when we aren't questioning God but are asking Him questions. Just like Joshua and Caleb, we will wonder where to go and what to do. We won't ask, "Why am I wandering, why am I so lost, and why is life so confusing?" Instead, we will ask, "What direction, Lord? I need you."

There is nothing greater than the Lord who is our guide. We must call on Him and cling to Him, because in the stillness of these moments, in the quietness of these questions, there is an answer. There is a way, and He will go with you and before you. He truly was the Israelites' fire by night and cloud by day. Will you let Him be yours? We experience miracles and His promises when we are obedient to God's unique calling and direction and trust that His power will place us in the right place at the right time. We experience His great and marvelous blessings when we walk where He tells us to walk and when we make the right choices in our lives. On this beautiful journey we can obtain His ultimate, beautiful will, if we learn to let go of yesterday. We can bloom new leaves. I think this was one major thing that Joshua realized.

The Israelites were free! God delivered them in incredible, miraculous ways. God took them out of bondage. After decades of imprisonment, they were free, but they were still prisoners in their minds. That was the origin of their doubt, fear and troubles. They couldn't let go of the place God took them from, and where there is doubt, there is always disobedience, but where there is faith, there is certainly obedience. In making the right choices, Joshua and Caleb saved an entire nation and its future, because they had faith and were obedient. They didn't have to say a word, and they didn't have to shout from the rooftops that they trusted God. They just walked onward. Let me tell you, friend, two of the most important things we can do to help us make the right decision is to be sensitive and faithful to the Lord.

That doesn't require us to methodically plan things out, wait for roadmaps to appear, or even hear the words "Go thou good and faithful servant" whispered in our ears. Sometimes our faith is simply in the going; sooner or later, we will face our Jordan and when we do, we must cross it. Otherwise, we will constantly face the same battles. Sometimes, as we walk in faith and as we get where God wants us to go, we have to come full circle. It's also important to know that God didn't just help the Israelites; they got up and helped themselves by following Him and His directions. Then they were taken to the Promised Land. We know where our help comes from, and we know where our guidance comes from. We know our cloud by day, and we know our light in the darkest of times. So go to it. Follow after it. Chase after it.

I think it's time that we need to stop trying to make decisions right and start making right decisions. Joshua realized this, and it is why he was chosen to lead a new generation into the Promised Land. He realized the great errors of his elders and their lack of faith. Abraham thought he was too old, did things the wrong way and had Ishmael. Moses struck the rock, but an entire generation doubted; many would have rather gone back into slavery instead of wander through the desert to the land of milk and honey. Many others settled for a land of cattle while some grew lazy and scared. But Joshua knew the way of the Lord. He listened to it. He adhered to it, and He clearly did something right. It's no coincidence that Joshua got to live out the promise while Moses died. It's no coincidence that Moses saw the Promised Land from a distance while Joshua partook in the land of milk and honey.

Joshua figured out the formula that will get us where God wants us. He realized we can't live the way we used to live. After all, we are not the people we used to be. Joshua realized the best question to ask is "What is the right thing to do?" He also realized that instead of asking God how much longer until it's over, we need to ask Him what He wants from us. I mean, the Israelites wandered for forty years in the desert, going through the same monotonous cycle of living. Let me ask you this: How many times do you want to walk in circles and for how long? How much energy do you want to exert while you wait for your promise of healing, while you wait for your "crown" like David did? If you are tired of wandering, walking in confusion, and making mistakes, perhaps I should take you to 2 Chronicles 11:16, which has good advice and shows the things you must act on. I do believe it is the right thing.

> And after them out of all the tribes of Israel such
> as set their hearts to seek the Lord God of Israel
> came to Jerusalem, to sacrifice unto the Lord God
> of their fathers.

Now, I know this scripture is peculiar, but it shows that devotion to, obedience to, and faith in God is a conscious "100 percent of the time" effort, not a half-hearted "when I have time." God wants your attention, and He is going to bless you for it.

Through the desert and the storms, on dry land and in flooding waters, when walking in circles and walking on water, between our meals of manna and those of fish and bread, and every trial we are facing in our own lives, God wants to change our perspective. This is because the ideologies that influence where we are and what we are going through sometimes need to be further broken down. We must learn to trust Him enough to see that suffering is sometimes for our perfection. Suffering removes from us what is detrimental and potentially keeping us from obtaining the promises of God.

We must be able and willing to take our focus off of "why and how long, Lord" and move it to "what and how much, Lord." This journey is the opportunity to show God that we can do what is right and that we are ready to obtain His promises. That is why it is important to try to make the right choices. He is driving out our impurities, and it isn't always what we take out of the situation, but how we respond to it. But then God drives us further through the desert, to the edge of His promise.

It took all of this for the Israelites to realize that God was the answer: the freeing, the running, the walking, the wall conquering, the enemy defeating, the parting waters, all of His miracles, and having their questions answered. It took trial and error and wandering and questioning. The children of Israel were taken to this place by God. Thank God when He takes you to a place of extreme irritation, and He most definitely will. He will take you to a moment when you are without solutions or answers, and it is dry and the skies feel like brass. When the sky has nothing to give you, the earth can do nothing for you, and death is all around you, thank Him for that moment, because that is exactly when God produces His mighty blessings. The Israelites were faced the Jordan River with God's promise within their grasp, waiting on the other side, and they were tired and some of them were beyond irritated. God took them to a place that didn't have the most comfortable conditions; they were in enemy territory, and the desert had become their resting place.

It's amazing to me that His ways are not our ways. God can get you to a place, right before the fulfillment of the promise, where He will give you time to rest, catch your breath, get a second wind, and the strength to go a little further. Thank God our ways are not His ways. Let me ask you this. Where is your resting place? Think about it for a moment. My resting place is on a beach somewhere, sitting next to the icy blue waters; walking the trails of Tennessee; or sitting on a cabin porch, reading a book. But God says no! He says:

> It's not the beach! It's not the trails in Tennessee that will give you rest. Your resting place is where there are no answers, and there is no other source. Your resting place is in me. When there's no other life, I will take you on a journey where your faith can grow and where you can move to a new level. Only then will I take you further into the things I have promised you.

It's astonishing to me that the Israelites had no water, and God gave them rest. They were exhausted, and God gave them rest. They had wandered and wandered for years and when they reached a breaking point, God gave them rest. They were irritable, and God gave them rest. They were in enemy territory, and God gave them rest. The same is true for you. It isn't where you go on vacation that will give you the rest and peace you need. It isn't the time away from work, although there is nothing wrong with those things. I am merely saying that regardless of where you go or what you do, the problems you face are still problems you face. They aren't geographically restricted, and they don't take time off. Anywhere you go, your problems may shrink, but they will still front you like the enemy they are.

Your rest comes solely from the Lord, and it is in Him, by Him and through Him that you can obtain rest on this long, enduring journey when you are surrounded by your enemies or sickness, whether you face death or divorce or anger and bitterness. But let us not grow "weary in well doing: for in due season we shall reap, if we faint not." Continue to do what is right in the eyes of the Lord, and He will continue to guide you and give you rest as you go about the rest of your journey, beyond the Jordan River and Jericho, and into the land of milk and honey. Always remember that the desert and the Jordan River were not the Israelites' destination, but their resting place so they could move forward. A much greater land awaited them. They had a far greater promise, a far greater destiny, and so do you, but find your rest in Christ Jesus along the way because you have not yet reached your destination. Continue to make the right choices, and He will give you rest, right before He leads the way into His promise.

Chapter 17

Promises, Property, and Problems

In Joshua 3:4, God speaks to His people in the way that He speaks to us today. He says, "You have not passed this way before." It makes me think about how strange our lives are. We face nearly the same things these Israelites faced. To Abraham, God promised his lineage the Promised Land, and the Israelites are at the shore of the river Jordan, nearly five hundred years later, finally on the cusp of something great. They have overcome so much, and everything looks so amazing! The sun is shining brightly where there was once all looked bleak. They are finally going to get their homeland!

They are going to obtain what the Lord had promised them. Joshua has to tell his people that they are going where they have not gone before. But the reason this is possible, that they can be confident that they will get there, and that they can jump into the unknown, is all centered and anchored around the Ark of the Covenant. It is all centered on His promise that this was to be their homeland.

My question to you is simple. I have asked myself this time and time again, and it is true to life. How can you face the unknown when you are staring at the property and the promise, yet there is a problem standing before you? That is the problem with the unknown! There always seem to be the most daunting, intimidating and terrifying things in our way. How can we continue forward in faith when what is in front of us seems so challenging? How can we be courageous when our problems seem to size us up?

The Jordan wasn't a small river; it was flooding and breaking barriers. The Israelites were staring at their problems in their seemingly most terrifying forms, and that is precisely how we often look at our problems. We think to ourselves, *If only the water levels were lower. If I could just find a safer way across. If I could find a little more familiarity, then I know I could make it.* But God says, "The water isn't as deep as you think. Your way isn't as spectacular as mine." Just like God told the Israelites, He is telling us:

> We are not going around. We are going through
> the waters into the unknown, and we are not
> going to do this because you are smart or because
> you had a plan. We are doing this because I will
> go before you. You have not passed this way
> before, but I will see you through. My promise
> will remain and my promise will protect you if
> you obey me, if you trust in me, and if you believe
> in my promises. You have not been this way, but
> you have me.

The Israelites had absolute security and confidence in God. The ark would go before them and split the waters miraculously.

How will you face the unknown? What will you do when you do not have the answers to your problems? When nobody knows, what will you do? Millions of Israelites jumped into the unknown without knowing what tomorrow would bring. How will you sleep at night when your life is full of uncertainty and variables that you can never fully control? We may not have been this way before, but we have a choice to make: we can grow arrogant and pretend that we know what is going on and what we should do. Or we can realize that we are on our way—headfirst, feet soaking wet, exhausted from walking, feet dragging behind us—into the unknown. Whether we acknowledge it or not, it is a fact of our lives and our very existence: we are meant to walk in faith and to walk blindly.

It is indicative of God's sovereignty that He knows what it takes for us to realize we were not created to hold back in fear. We were not created to take the safe route, but to know who our God is and to leap into the unknown and say:

> God, I don't know what tomorrow holds, but I know who holds tomorrow. I know I rest in the palms of your hands. I know you can cause the storms to cease. I know you can walk on water. I know you can guide me through the desert. I know you can remove obstacles. But I also know you can take me through, so I am going to launch into the depths of the unknown, and I am going to embrace the risks and throw caution to the wind. Life is short, so I'm going to make it matter!

The truth is, we can make it matter—not by staying frozen to the shore, not by refusing to let our feet get wet or to get uncomfortable, but by leaping into the space that only God controls. We can make it matter by clinging to God's promises and forsaking the problems before us. We haven't come this far to turn back around. We haven't come this far to let fear and hurt and worry to keep us from obtaining what the Lord has for us. We haven't stood on the shores as alive as ever to play it safe. We haven't gone through all that we have to muddy up the shores.

I can only imagine the miracles that we could testify about if we jumped into the unknown. I wonder how many diseases would have come and gone. I wonder how many marriages and relationships would be saved and how many people would make it through horrible pain, agony, strife, and difficulty. Do you know how much you have gone through? And you are still here! It isn't to sit on the shores. It isn't to cower away from your problems. Life is but a vapor, and we will die before we know it. It is here today and gone tomorrow. It is time to dive into the unknown, because we were made to follow Jesus. We were made to follow the faithful One, the one who has never failed us yet, the one who makes a way when there is absolutely no way. What's the worst that could happen? We lose something behind us? We miss out on something that is behind us? You can't lose Him! You can't miss out on God if you follow Him! We can't remember the former things. We can't look behind us, because God is doing a new thing. Oh if the Israelites would have realized that the moment God took them out of slavery!

I sometimes think God brings us to the shores of His promises just to ask us the million-dollar question. "Do you see it? Can you feel it?" And I ask you the same question: do you see it? If so, then I believe you will jump. God is doing something unlike anything He has ever done before. He is doing things you have not seen with your eyes. You've not gone this way before. We share a faith with the Israelites, and the same God who was with them is with us, but God has proven and shown Himself in a far more profound way! He is not a box like the Ark of the Covenant; He is the fulfillment of all the miraculous things within it. He is the fulfillment of the miraculous events in the wilderness, the miracles on the water, and He is the fulfillment of promises. God now walks among us, and He tells us to follow Him into the unknown and all the way to the place where He wants us to be, because the God who provided for our ancestors thousands of years ago will not stop providing for us today. What does jumping into the unknown mean to you?

Let me tell you, circumstances don't nullify God's promise. It doesn't matter how high the waters are or how frequent the obstacles. His promises are true. His promises are yes and amen. His promises are never negated. Could it be that the journey to that promise the journey through the problems, is the miracle that takes us to His promise? The journey there is a miracle in and of itself. Through every promise God gives, there is a test that seems impassible. I encourage you to keep hold of the promise God has given to you. Adhere to the words He has spoken, and embrace His ways. You can walk through the water and not get wet. Don't dwell where you are. Don't dabble on the shore. Do not doubt Him.

Joshua trusted God, and He talked to God. He prayed! It's vital to know that prayer is our movement toward God, which ultimately becomes our movement toward the place He wants us to go, and it will draw us back to God! It's the circle of life. Through the journey and the destination, God will bless us with more of Him. He has promises for us to obtain. The Israelites obtained the Promised Land, and the disciples reached the other side. God fulfilled His promise, but first He got them to realize that all of it was secondary to Him, and that at the end of God's promises, there is always praise, because God always fulfills His promises.

Chapter 18

He'll Get You There His Way

"And Joshua rose early in the morning; and they removed from Shittim, and came to Jordan, he and all the children of Israel, and lodged there before they passed over. And it came to pass after three days, that the officers went through the host; And they commanded the people, saying, When ye see the ark of the covenant of the Lord your God, and the priests the Levites bearing it, then ye shall remove from your place, and go after it. Yet there shall be a space between you and it, about two thousand cubits by measure: come not near unto it, that ye may know the way by which ye must go: for ye have not passed this way heretofore. And Joshua said unto the people, sanctify yourselves: for tomorrow the Lord will do wonders among you."

—Joshua 3:1–5 (KJV)

After all these years, all the heartache and pain, the nights of waiting, unrest, confusion, and uncertainty, and after every obstacle they had faced, the Israelites had almost made it through. They were right on the brink of their promise from God. They could almost taste the food that would no longer be manna from heaven. They could smell the sweet essence of this wonderful land and after these treacherous years of aimlessly wandering, the time had finally come when God wanted them to cross over the river Jordan into the Promised Land—the land He had promised to Abraham hundreds of years earlier, the land for which they'd made this entire journey. All of this was possible because Joshua believed. He birthed hope within the Israelites, and that is why God chose Him to be Israel's new leader.

But Joshua also knew he and the Israelites could not enter the Promised Land unless the Lord helped them, because between their camp and the land that God had promised them was the river Jordan. This wasn't just your ordinary river. It was large and, as far as we know, there were no bridges, boats, or rafts to help them get across. You see, the Israelites again needed help; they needed something that human hands couldn't make. They really needed God's help. I wonder if the memories of them flashed back to the moment God had moved on their behalf to help them cross over the Red Sea forty years earlier. I wonder if Joshua had a smile on his face, remembering the glory days when God told Him what would happen. I wonder if he worshipped, believing in the promises and might of his God. I wonder if he thanked the great Yahweh for being the way. I wonder if he thanked the I Am for being the was, is, and always will be.

When you face high waters again, will you worship the Lord? Will you remember the things He has already done for you, the trials He resolved for you, the pit from which He yanked you, the life He breathed into your dead, hopeless situation? Will your faith grow stronger as you remember the stories of healing and restoration? Will you trust that He took you to a time and place such as this to work in you and for you? God loves you too much to leave you on the shore. He loves you too much to leave you in the water, and He loves you far too much to tease you with what is on the horizon. God will get you where you're supposed to go. He will certainly get you there, but it will be in a way you never expected. God will do miracles, but He will use ways that never occurred to you.

He healed a man who was blind from birth with some spit

and a little clay before telling him to go and wash in the pool of
Siloam. He healed a lame man without using the troubled waters.
In fact, His word alone changed everything. He spoke the miracle
into existence: Jesus told him to rise, take up his bed, and walk.
He healed a woman who had an issue of blood for twelve years;
after years of exhausting every avenue of doctors and down to
her last hope, she reached out to Jesus and was made whole by
her faith alone. In the middle of a busy crowd, Jesus healed her
and told her to go in peace. There is something similar to all
three miracles. Jesus said, "Go." He said, "Rise and walk." He
said, "Go in peace." In all three of these incredible miracles, God
told people to move and to take action. The very same God who
told them to move is the exact same God who spoke to Joshua
"When ye see the ark of the covenant of the Lord your God, and
the priests the Levites bearing it, then ye shall remove from your
place, and go after it."

Do you see it? God had already given Joshua the promise.
Actually, He gave it to all of Israel, and yet, time and time again,
obstacles stood before them. Still, all God did was tell them to
go. The waters were vast and scary. The waters were still flowing.
The trek to the other side was treacherous. Even when you cannot
see Him, something keeps you from getting what you need, or
a crowd stands in your way, miracles are there for you. God's
promises lie on the other side, and nothing can keep you from
obtaining them. It's not the troubled waters that heal us or luck
that gets us to His promises, but faith and obedience in God that
will allow us to experience Him moving God firsthand, in such
a marvelous way.

God could have told Joshua to walk around the Jordan to
reach what was promised to him. I don't know how long the river
was, but I imagine Joshua and the Israelites would have accepted
this suggestion or maybe even preferred it. They had walked for
forty years, and I doubt, in their minds, that it was a big deal to
walk some more at that point. A huge, terrifying wall waited in

the distance anyway. They looked at the flowing waters, maybe longing to find a way around the river. I wonder if any of them said to Joshua or even cried unto God, "If we can only find a clear path to cross over, we can make it." Is that not how we in our natural, finite minds would respond? Wouldn't we look for other means to pass over or reach the other side? Wouldn't we first discard God's scary ways and try to fix our own problems? The Israelites probably accepted the extended time it would take to get to the Promised Land in the distance. They had waited forty long years for a promise that was unfulfilled. Time probably had very little value to them anymore.

I put myself in Joshua's shoes here. I look at things from my perspective every time I study biblical characters. In that moment, if I were Joshua, I probably would have had a little shouting match with God. I would have said, "You want me to do what?" And as God tried to interrupt my questioning of Him, I would say "That's crazy, God. No way, no thanks." I would tell myself that the people would listen to me because the faith of their ancestors was fickle, and I would yell to them from my high horse, "All right, folks. Pack up the tents, untie the cattle, and gather your stuff because we're going around."

If some of you are honest with yourselves, you too would react like this, and I dare to say some of you have at one time or another. You are alone in your prayer time and ask God, "Really? This is how you want to do it? I'm just trying to be safe and careful, but you do not want this done the way I want it. You don't make any sense."

And He pricks your heart, saying, "My ways are not your ways, my child."

Through your desperate, scared tears, you say, "But God, can I …"

And He interrupts, saying, "No." God already knows our questions, and so He has the answers before we finish.

But you persist: "God, I'm tired of facing all of this, can I …"

As He interrupts again: "No, my child. Just go. Do as I tell you. It will be worth it."

We've all faced hard times. We've been scared to move. We've wondered if there was any point in holding on, and we've asked God for an alternative route. But God says:

No. That's not going to work anymore. Walking around isn't going to work anymore. Avoiding confrontation isn't going to work. Wavering faith isn't going to be a part of this journey any longer. Sleepless nights and broken dreams and unfulfilled promises aren't going to be a part of your life. Living in hurt and pain isn't going to work. Walking around isn't going to work anymore. You're going through!

God said this to Joshua and the Israelites. He said, "When the ark of the covenant (the promise) moves, then you pack up and follow."

Through the Israelites and their entire journey and through you and yours, God is trying to get your attention. He is saying:

You'll make it in the most unlikely way possible. You may even get a little wet, your hair may be a little grayer, you may be tired, and you may come out a different person, but you're going to make it because you have been faithful and because I am with you. Because it is my promise, it is going to be *my* way. It'll get uncomfortable, it'll be nerve wracking at times, but *you are* going to make it!

God has so much in store for us, if we will only learn to trust His every word and obey His every direction. We serve a great God who fulfills His miracles through the unlikeliest of scenarios.

He finds great joy in those who trust and serve Him simply for who He is. He delights Himself in us and I believe He relishes in the opposition. He relishes in opportunities that show us just how truly big our God is. In moments when mankind says it can't be done, He longs for us to say, "Not me, but you, Lord. I can't, but you can. Not my way, but yours." Those are the words we speak, when we are at the end of ourselves, that allow Him to step in, in a way only He can, and do what only He can.

I imagine God speaking in that moment. The cold waters invited the Israelites in. The sun cast shadows over the Promised Land, turning the city line into bright colors; the heat bore down on the Israelites. Sweat beat down Joshua's brow as birds chirped in the distance. I imagine the Lord said to Joshua: "You've trusted me all this time and I have entrusted you. You've agreed and walked with me. You haven't questioned my method yet. Don't change that now." And I imagine Joshua lifting his hands as he cried to God in worship before he properly prepared and directed the ark of the covenant's movement forward.

They obeyed God's unique direction. The priests carried the ark of the covenant down to the edge of the water, and the Israelites followed them. But as the priests reached the river and put their feet in the water, did they wonder how they would all cross over. God told Joshua that He would make a clear path through the river. Now if you ask me, they would need a lot of faith to believe that a deep, wide river would open up and let them cross through on dry ground, wouldn't they? It's beautiful to know, though, that God is pleased when we do what He asks us to do, even though it may seem difficult or even impossible. It may be hard for us to get our hopes up, but God will always help us do whatever He asks.

The priests put their feet into the Jordan River, hands clinging to the ark. The water upriver stopped flowing, although below where they stood, the water kept on flowing. It wasn't long before the riverbed in front of them had been drained dry, and they were able to miraculously cross over. After forty long years of wandering in the wilderness and living in tents, the Israelites had endured and were finally on the other side, in the Promised Land. The land was so fertile they called it the land of milk and honey. It was full of grain and tons of other things to eat. They didn't need manna from heaven anymore, so it ceased to fall. There were no more breadcrumbs. God cared for them in other ways. They didn't need tents because they were no longer a traveling people. God had given them residence. Their faith had taken them there, right on the shores of the Jordan River. God had assuredly helped them cross over, but there was one more thing in their way. One final act of faith, destroying the walls of Jericho, stood between them and their promise. These at one time would have been walls of hopelessness, only now, they knew in whom they believed.

The value of faith is that it is so strong, it can move landscapes, change situations, remove obstacles, and turn an unlikely situation into something positive. Nothing can get in the way to stop you from obtaining a miracle or God's promise to you. When the Lord tells you to move—regardless of the time, situation, or scenario; whether it makes little or no sense; and regardless of how scary it is or how much faith it requires—be obedient to Him. He has a purpose, and God isn't in the business of teasing His children, whom He loves. He isn't interested in games or suffering, for that matter. God wants to prepare you for what He has promised you and the miracles he will perform for you. God wants to show you how big and powerful He is. God is interested in you. He wants you to realize just how much you need Him. He wants you to say "not me, but you," and He wants you to say "I can't," so that He can smile down on you and say "I can." He is looking for obedience and faith in Him, and He is waiting for you to open your ears to Him and listen so He can say go. Because when God says go, a miracle is taking place, and He is directing you to the other side.

What does the Lord require you to do? What is He asking of

you? Is He whispering "go, your faith has made thee whole"? Is He telling you to take up your bed and walk? Perhaps He is asking you to do something more pertinent to your situation—make amends to someone who has offended you, forgive someone, contact that friend you haven't spoken to in years. Perhaps He is telling you to give more. You can insert whatever you'd like if you feel Him pressing something on your heart. But perhaps this thing that you could fill in here is your Jordan River, which you must cross in order to get to the other side. If it is, be obedient to the Lord and trust God with your whole heart. You will get wet, but the Lord, like the ark of the covenant, will go before you, and you will enter new territory. You will no longer need manna to get by. God will provide for you in many other ways. Greater things await if you simply go. Be obedient and watch as He removes the fear, doubt, and worry and creates a clear, unquestioned path for you. Watch as you enter into His promise.

Chapter 19

The Walls of Hopelessness

"Now Jericho was straightly shut up because of the children of Israel: none went out and none came in. And the Lord said unto Joshua, "See, I have given into thine hand Jericho, and the king thereof, and the mighty men of valor.""

—Joshua 6:1–2 (KJV)

"By faith the walls of Jericho fell down, after they were compassed about seven days."

—Hebrews 11:30 (KJV)

The title of this chapter hits home to many of us, doesn't it? I assume we've all run dead smack into roadblocks and giant walls that have completely destroyed our morale at times. We have crashed into them and fallen onto our backs. It seems like everywhere we turn in our Christian walk, we are faced with impossible and hopeless obstacles where the outcome is unfavorable. If it isn't slavery, giants, stormy waters, an army on your back, or wandering in a wilderness without food or water, we face insurmountable walls of hopelessness. I don't know what yours is; walls are almost always what stand between you and the other side with your promise from God. Maybe it's healing you need; maybe you lost your job, and God has spoken to you about providing another one. Maybe you feel abandoned, and you are waiting for someone to come along and let you realize that life will not always be that way.

I do not know the problems that everyone faces or promises you have been given, but I do know we all face them. We have and we always will, but I also know that beyond these walls are the beginning of a great move of God and the start of His fulfilled promise. If we can only make it through, past, or beyond them, God will have something beautiful for us. Sadly, many of us duck tail and run when things overwhelm us. We have to tilt our heads as far back as we can to see the top of these walls and so much runs through our minds. We get discouraged and our "fight for it" attitude turns into a "run from it" attitude. The altitude of our obstacles in comparison to the height of our faith becomes just as high and just as wide as the wall itself and if we aren't careful, the chasm can become far too wide for us to bridge. Walls are huge! Walls are scary! Walls look unconquerable. Walls are downright discouraging! Walls are always in the way. Some walls look downright impenetrable. I remember years ago, my brother-in-law asked me, "What happens when an unstoppable force is met with an unmovable, impenetrable object?" Truthfully, I didn't have a real answer, so I sarcastically said, "It moves around it."

That question and my answer stuck with me for years, and until I wrote this chapter, I did not realize how true it was. When we face an obstacle, we must move around it. That is exactly what Joshua and the Israelites did and how they obeyed God. The good thing is that we are called to do the exact same thing, and it is of great value to know that we aren't alone! We never have been, and neither were they. Something far greater was at work for them, and the same Spirit who helped them at their walls of hopelessness will help you at yours. The same Spirit who guided them through the wilderness will guide you through yours. The same Spirit who provided for them will provide for you, and the same God who led them to a place of victory will lead you to yours.

As described in these particular scriptures, Joshua and Hebrews, the walls were formidable obstacles, especially for those one hundred thousand wilderness wanderers. But God, their promise giver, their fire by night and cloud by day, had led them there. The breadcrumbs and all roads led to that very moment, and God had given them distinct instructions for conquering the city of Jericho. Read the passages in Joshua chapter 6, and you will see how little sense they seem to make. Against overwhelming odds, though, Joshua led the people of Israel in their conquest of the Promised Land, beginning with the strange and miraculous battle of Jericho.

They had been walking for so long; they walked through water and didn't get wet. Now they faced this giant thing in their way, and there was no time for rest or reevaluating. They were told to walk and they did just that. They walked again! How annoying that must have felt to them. It was Joshua's strong faith that caused him to obey though, no matter how illogical God's commands might have seemed. Thank God Joshua was not Mr. Spock, the man of logic in the TV show *Star Trek*. He was the man of faith and obedience. In fact, obedience, faith, and dependence on the Lord made Him one of Israel's finest leaders, and Joshua set an incredibly brave example for us to follow.

The wall of Jericho was an impenetrable force for any army that tried to overtake the city. Before the attacking troops dealt with the giant wall, they would have to navigate their way across a twenty-seven-foot-wide, nine-foot-deep pit that lined the outer edges of the city. Then there was the wall itself—pure stone, seventeen feet high and five feet wide. If the attacking army managed to get that far without being shot down by archers, all that was left was to defeat the well-trained Canaanite army that was waiting within. This was the reality faced by Joshua, the young leader, and his ragtag Israelite army. The Israelites, who had seen an entire generation live and die wandering through the desert, were tired, hungry, and facing what seemed like an impossible situation.

This was no normal city, and the wall wasn't just some simple wall of defense. There was so much more than that. It was about five miles west of Jordan; it was the most important city in the Jordan Valley and the strongest fortress in all of Canaan. The wall and the city were the key to western Palestine. The Israelites had to destroy and conquer this wall and city to make it the rest of the way. If you read the scriptures, you'll see the city was taken in a very remarkable manner by the Israelites—a unique way and one only God would use.

Now, I haven't lived very long, but I've lived long enough to know that running into walls is a part of life. The bigger the wall, the more hopeless the situation can seem. The large walls of sickness, loss, divorce, addiction pop up all around us, and they seem impenetrable. Just like the walls of Jericho, these walls hardly stand alone. The walls of our lives are often accompanied by deep pits of pain, suffering, and despair and, all the while, an army of hopelessness attacks us on every side. People ask these questions all the time: If God loves me so much and is so powerful, how can He allow these walls to pop up around me? How can He allow all of this suffering? Why does such suffering even exist? The questions go on and on.

I don't pretend to have the answer to any of these questions or to understand how deep, dark, and painful your suffering has been. I simply suggest that God does His best work during seemingly hopeless situations. In the Bible, I read about people who faced seemingly hopeless situations. I cannot find a single person who walked faithfully with God and lived out God's promises without first facing a hopeless situation of his or her own. This is true not only the scriptures but in our world today.

Adam and Eve ruined paradise by inviting sin and death into a perfect world. A hopeless case. Joseph was betrayed by his brothers due to his pride and thrown into a prison. A hopeless case. Moses was cornered on the banks of the Red Sea with the most powerful army in the world breathing down His neck. A hopeless case. Gideon was three hundred against three hundred thousand. David stood across the valley from a blood-thirsty giant after practicing with only a bear and a lion. Esther was a woman who tried to gain a word with a prideful king. Daniel's roommate was a lion; his friends were thrown in an oven. Jonah was terrible at his job and got stuck in a whale. Peter was a coward. Paul was imprisoned. The five thousand had no food. Lazarus was deader than dead. Timothy was way too young. Abraham was far too old. The prodigal son was stupid and impatient. The walls of Jericho were too big, too strong, too scary, and too dangerous. Jesus was humiliated, beaten and bruised, crucified, and buried in a tomb—burying all hope of the hoped-for revolution for thousands of years. Everybody was willing to close the book on these stories. The end. Game over.

But if there is one thing we learn from the scriptures, it is that God loves an underdog story and a good comeback. We can never place a period where God has placed a comma. God shows up exactly when all other options have been worn out, we've exhausted all efforts, when circumstances can't get worse, everything else has failed and all your fickle attempts have made matters worse. Joseph became second in command; the Red Sea parted; Gideon won without lifting even one weapon; Goliath fell to the ground and his head ended up on a plate; Esther spoke with confidence and the king listened; Daniel tamed the lion, and the oven felt like nothing more than room temperature; Jonah arrived, preached, and Nineveh repented; Peter became the rock; Paul rejoiced in the Lord; twelve baskets full were left over; Lazarus was just kidding; Timothy built a church; Abraham and Sarah changed their names and built a family; the prodigal son came back home to a party; and the giant walls of Jericho came tumbling down. Jesus Christ, the Son of God, pulled off the resurrection, defeating sin and death, and the creation that had been doomed so many years ago was now restored for all time!

With God, what seems like a hopeless situation is not only possible, it is favorable, because only God can turn a mess into a message. Only God can turn a trial into a triumph, a test into a testimony, and a victim into a victory. His power is made perfect in weakness. So, let us rejoice in our trials and hold unswervingly to the hope we profess. Cling to the God who promised, the God, who already has and will continue to see us through, because He who promised *is* faithful, *was* faithful and *always will be* faithful. It does not matter how hopeless the situation may seem, or how little sense God's ways seem to make, or the steps He tells us to take, or the instruction He gives. It does not matter if it seems that His response is delayed, our prayers have fallen on deaf ears, or His hands cannot reach far enough. He will work. He will move, and it will certainly result in victory. It will all be worth it.

God gave Joshua the strangest of instructions. He told Joshua right away that He had given him the city of Jericho. He told him specifically to take all the Israelites and walk around the city once a day for six days; then on the seventh day, they were to walk around seven times and blow their trumpets and shout. Nothing in these scriptures makes any sense—not the instructions from God, not the logic, and definitely not walking around aimlessly. I kept asking myself what the point was as I read this story. Why did God tell them to blow their horns? Why did they walk around seven times on the seventh day? This was supposed to be a war. You read about the dangers inside and outside this wall; you read that everything was on the line; and you expect a massacre of the one hundred thousand Israelites and their feeble foot soldiers. What was the point of these distinct instructions? I truly do not have an answer, but I do not believe it had anything to do with the marching or with God's methods of walking. The trumpets did not blow magical power from within. It didn't have anything to do with speed, agility or the positioning of the Israelites. It didn't even have to do with their intelligence.

Those aren't the things that led to the destruction of the wall and the conquering of Jericho. But they most certainly worked, because on the seventh day, Joshua had so much faith in God and His ability that he reminded the Israelites of the promise God had spoken to them before it was even fulfilled. In the unlikeliest of situations, Joshua said, "Shout; for the Lord hath given you the city." The most important thing to note though is the Israelites waited and obeyed the Lord's instruction. Moments later, they moved and shouted as the walls fell flat and opened up the gateway to Canaan's land. That giant wall became nothing more than a giant stepping stone, a monument, a remembrance of what they had overcome to enter into God's promise and destiny that He had orchestrated for hundreds upon hundreds of years.

They walked around the seventh time; they shouted and the city fell flat, just as God had promised His people. But none of this would have been possible if Joshua, God's personally chosen leader and the Israelites, had not obeyed God and His unusual instructions. If the Israelites did not have the faith to trust God in every moment and trust His wisdom and abilities, they never would have made it through that city, and the walls would not have fallen. But by faith, the walls of Jericho fell down. Joshua had enough faith to be obedient, enough confidence to lead, and enough humbleness to defer his plans and his ways to those of the Lord. He knew that regardless of the outcome or the method, God's ways were higher than His. It was not about God's strange directions; it was about faith and obedience to Him. It's true that God allows us to go through adversity so that we can learn. It isn't always what we take out of the situation, it's the way we respond to it that is the lesson. By the way we respond, the way we grow, and by the way we grow, the closer we draw to God. The greater understanding we have of God and the ways He speaks, the closer we draw to God, the greater the reward.

Joshua responded as we should. He responded accordingly to the adversity thrown his way. He faithfully obeyed The Lord step by step and word by word. He never argued with God, never questioned or bargained with Him, didn't give God a contingency plan in order to obey. Joshua didn't cower away from giants, he didn't give in to the crowds of doubt and he didn't fear starvation or dying of thirst because He knew The Lord who promised them land and who said He came to heal and deliver them would provide for them up until the very end. Joshua listened to God. He adhered to Him. Joshua was faithful, obedient and responsive to God and He reaped great rewards and obtained the promises of God because of it. I believe it is time us as a church and individually take a page, both literally and metaphorically, from the book of Joshua; The faithful follower, the successful leader and a great pinnacle of faith. Though Joshua was not specifically mentioned in the Hall of Faith, it was because of his faith as a leader that Hebrews 11:30 was ever made possible and the entering of Canaan land was even a part of such a rich history; and it will be because of your faith that God will do what He told you He will do. Be pliable to His direction, obedient to His word and faithful in your walk and watch as God does great and marvelous things.

Joshua walked when the Spirit said walk, and he was often tasked with walking the unknown path. He had to go when the Spirit told Him to. He spoke when the Lord gave him utterance and as an obedient follower of faith, he also became a great leader in our faith, an incredible leader of the Israelites, and a recipient of God's promise that originated all the way back in the days of Abraham. Due to this act of faith on Joshua's part, he was able to destroy walls, conquer giants, silence doubters, and obtain the promises of God! Your greatest struggle can turn into your greatest victory if you choose to not give up. Keep the fight, keep the faith, and keep being obedient! We often subconsciously believe that faith is there to make things easy, and we only want to walk in faith if it is fun or easy. But the truth is, walking in faith in tumultuous times of life, when the direction is a little too clouded, probably isn't our idea of fun and entertaining. Often, we want the discomfort and risk to be removed. We prefer not to have to guess the outcome, and before we make a move, we want God to make it crystal clear what will happen. Joshua understood that faith does not mean going from road sign to road sign on a straight path, following their direction and avoiding the detours they warn us about. Faith is more like wandering along a winding road of wilderness with no sense of direction other than the steps God orders you to take and the fire by night to guide you.

Joshua also knew that if left to ourselves, we will never get to where God wants us, because we will want the journey to take place in a typical, natural, safe way. Often, we want to follow the road signs and hug the guard rails to make it safely to the other side. But thank the Lord, we serve an unnatural God who will push us onto the unbeaten path and get us where He said He would in a beautiful and adventurous way. He will get us there in a way that reminds us only He can do it and only His way works. To truly sum this up, faith is going where we are supposed to go when we don't know the direction and we have to get there in a way no person has gone before. Sometimes, it is discouraging. Sometimes we will mess up, but God's way is definitely more exhilarating, absolutely more adventurous, and always, always worth it. Patience pays off, and patience is taught, learned, and earned in faith. Joshua trusted the Lord. He knew God was not a liar. He knew God was fighting for him. He knew due to the promise God had given them, the Israelites were an unstoppable force.

What happens when an unstoppable force is met with an unmovable, impenetrable object in your life? The answer is, move around it; let it become not a roadblock, but a stepping stone. Let it become not a distraction, but a distant memory of victory. Be obedient, have faith in God, and watch as the problems fall away around you. Watch and shout in victory as you enter into the promise and the miracle that has been promised to you for so long.

Chapter 20

The Other Side and How We Made It

Sometimes we want to see and experience what is on the other side before we ever make a move forward and before we listen to the pulling of our hearts. However, God rarely shows us the other side before He has tested us and prepared us for it. But when we are ready for it and when God's time has finally arrived, He will show us His blessings! He will reveal to us what awaits us, and it will be things our eyes have not yet seen. It will make the entire journey and all of the heartache worth it. On the other side, we will no longer be able to just get by. On the other side, there will be no more doubt and worry. On the other side, we will experience healing, blessings, and miracles and so much more that God wants to do for us.

He has brought you so far and made a way time and time again for you to reach the other side. He moved on your behalf when you didn't know where to go. He moved landscapes when you didn't have any strength left. He showed you grace and had mercy when you messed up, and when you realized you didn't deserve a thing, He gave you more than you ever expected. God loves you. He has loved you all along, and He will prove it when you see the ways in which He will move and reward you for being faithful and walking according to His word.

The Lord will bless you for doing the right thing and making the right choices; for holding on when others told you to let it go; for pressing forward when others turned around. Worship the Lord for He has done great things, and He is to be praised. Worship Him as He brings His plan to fruition.

There was definitely more than met the eye on the other side of the storm in Matthew, and there was more than met the eye on the shores of Jordan. It was hidden by the high waters in both stories. Sometimes we don't look very hard for things we don't believe will happen. But God didn't give us these dreams, this hope, and these promises for no reason. He wants to do something great with them, but we must be prepared. We must steady our hearts, be ready, and prepare our eyes to see what He is doing and is going to do.

Just like the Promised Land, what lies on the other side for you is more than you could ever imagine, and it is better than you thought it would be. It will be overflowing and plentiful. On the other side is God's will. On the other side is His blessing and His promise that He promised to you, and though things turned sour and ugly, though you stumbled and failed, God didn't. God's promise didn't change, and God was faithful all the way through to the other side. There is no more manna from heaven, because there is something better. There are no more tents and wandering, because God has given you a dwelling place and a residence. There is no more slavery, because you are free.

The other side is exactly where He wants you to be. It's exactly where He will get you and where His promises await you. It is by faith and God's guidance that you made it. Everything else—the in-between, the meantime, all of it—was merely to draw you closer to Him, that He may bless you and fulfill your promises. So cling to the Lord, even on the other side.

How Did We Get Here?

Often, when we will finally make it across our Jordan River, beyond the walls, and to the other side, we are left in awe at the moment in which we seem to be frozen. In our very presence is exactly what the Lord ordained, and we realize just how faithful and wonderful He truly is. We will experience unspeakable joy. We will walk a new walk. We will live and walk with purpose and meaning and dwell where God desires, and it will be the most beautiful thing you will ever experience. We may be so enthralled with the wonderful emotions of finally making it or finally obtaining it, that we can sometimes ask ourselves, How did we get here? How did we get to this thrilling and exciting moment again? How did we get to this place when things looked ugly?

Aside from faith, perseverance, and obedience, it had nothing to do with your ability, but everything to do with His. It didn't look like it would heal, but God stepped in. The walls looked unconquerable, but God moved. We weren't sure how we would make it, but God made a way. His promise looked unlikely and the way seemed impossible, but God! He proved and continues to prove that He is for us and He is fighting for us, because He wants us to draw close to Him and make it to the other side. He revels in our longing for Him, and when we are faced with difficult situations in our families, our ailments, and our relationships—when the storms of life are raging on all around us—we must call upon the One who is for us! We must hold onto the One who will carry us victoriously to the other side.

What Is the Point in Holding On?

Let me tell you. When you stand on the promises of God—whether in a rocking boat; stormy, flooding waters; or the middle of a dry and barren land—you are always standing on good ground. There will be times on the rough side of the mountain when we just have to agree with God. There will be no other choice but to agree with Him on His promises. When we are hurting and confused, we must agree with God. When we can't put the pieces together and we don't understand what is going on, we must agree with God. In Hebrews 11:17–19, Abraham did just that. By faith, Abraham offered his only son as a sacrifice to God, knowing that it was through Isaac that God's promise would be fulfilled. Abraham knew in whom he believed. He knew that God would raise Isaac up, even from death. When nothing else made sense, He agreed with God. He agreed with His character. He agreed with His promise.

The God who met the Israelites in the middle of their journey and the middle of their storm met them on the other side. The same God who meets you in the middle will meet you on the other side. The point in holding on is that miracles happen on both sides of the storm; they happen on both sides of your journey; and they happen in between! God moves on our behalf! He shows us His power and strength, and He prepares us for what He has planned for us. We were not called to live on the shore, to steer the boat, to wander aimlessly, to moan, groan, complain, and waver in our faith. We were called to so much more. We were called to something higher. We were called to cling to Him as He leads us. We were made to experience God in all His godliness. If you can persevere, if you can ready your heart and mind for the battles you will face. If you can continue to trust and believe what God promised you, He will get you there, and He certainly will not disappoint.

That is the point in holding on! We serve a big God with big plans for you and me. We serve a God who wants to fulfill His blessings and promises to us! We serve a God who is faithful until the very end and beyond that, a God who <u>does</u> better than your best and knows the perfect way to <u>help you succeed</u>.

We serve a God who is sometimes a mystery but always rewarding. He shows tough love, but makes us tough and fulfills His promises when we wonder if He ever will. God is our rock, and in Him lies the power to change everything. Are you willing to hold on all the way to the other side?

About the Author

Seth Ramey resides in the land of champions, where they bleed scarlet and gray. After many years of journaling and posting blogs, he is pursuing his dream and passion for writing. The middle child in a family of seven, he has a heart for children, young adults, and missions.

CPSIA information can be obtained
at www.ICGtesting.com
Printed in the USA
LVOW12*2022120517
534340LV00002B/2/P